the gospels
as a
mandala
of wisdom

By Geddes MacGregor

the gospels as a mandala of wisdom

*This publication made possible with
the assistance of the Kern Foundation*

**The Theosophical Publishing House
Wheaton, Illinois U.S.A.
Madras, India/London, England**

Library of Congress Cataloging in Publication Data

MacGregor, Geddes.
    The Gospels as a mandala of wisdom.
    "A Quest original"—T.p. verso.
    Bibliography: p.
    1. Bible. N. T. Gospels—Criticism, interpretation, etc. 2. Jesus
Christ—Theosophical interpretations, I. Title.
BS2555,2.M25   226'.06   81-53010
ISBN 0-8356-0554-X   (pbk.)   AACR2

Printed in the United States of America

CONTENTS

INTRODUCTION

This little book is intended for those who are interested in the life of Jesus and may wish to see how the Ancient Wisdom that has come to us through the ages can shed light on what the Gospels tell us of his Person and his work. When modern biblical scholarship (a difficult and technical study) is illumined by the insights of the Ancient Wisdom, the meaning of the Gospels is immensely clarified.

The concept of the biography as we understand it today was unknown until fairly recent times. The Evangelists, like others in the ancient world engaged in depicting the life and work of great prophets, teachers, heroes, and saints, wrote impressionistically. Nowadays, when we read the biography of a person such as, say, Shaw or Tolstoy or Florence Nightingale, we expect the biographer to have researched his or her material in such a way as to be able to tell us plainly the exact date of birth, the location, the date of graduation, if any, the date of every letter cited, and even the minute details about the kind of dress Florence Nightingale wore at Scutari and the length of Shaw's beard. We demand detail and accuracy. The concept among the ancients was quite different. They sought to give a vivid picture of their subject's personality, how he was perceived by others and how he saw himself, how he characteristically behaved, and what was the principal aim of his life. From such a standpoint it does not much matter whether Jesus did this today and that tomorrow or the other way around. It certainly could not much matter whether he was tall or short. The important thing, from this standpoint, is what *kinds* of words and acts were typical of him. The writer remembers or has been told a striking incident. Down it goes in the narrative. Its place in the sequence matters very much less than the vividness of its illustrative function. This may not be necessarily always the case, of course. Sometimes the writer may account the order of events vital to what he is trying to do. Generally, however, it is not nearly so important as we account it today.

Telling the parables in precisely the circumstances suggested would not have seemed of much consequence to people in the ancient world, so long as they represented the way Jesus taught and the illustrations he was in the habit of employing. Many of his characteristic utterances might be collected and pasted together, as today we might splice one piece of film to another in constructing a cinepicture. Here is our hero walking down his driveway, then jumping into his blue Ford, and shortly afterwards we see him stopping to greet his friend, a pedestrian in a brown suit. Historical research might discover that at no time when he had a blue car did his friend have a brown suit, although he frequently met his friend and talked with him like that. For most of us such details would not matter; only fastidious historians would complain. In the ancient world people would have cared much less about such detail, so long as they felt they could rely on the general veracity of the picture. So the Sermon on the Mount, for example, could very well be constructed, as many scholars contend, out of a collection of typical utterances that seemed to the compiler of the same sort and therefore suitable for pasting together, as we might paste together in an album a collection of photographs all relating to the same general subject and so having coherence of a kind.

The editorial conscience in the ancient world was different from ours in other ways, too. A story might be introduced by way of symbolically presenting the character of the subject. That is not to say that this was done in any very consistent way. The editorial process was often complex. Nevertheless, the general intent was to provide a vivid portrait such that anyone who had known the subject would acclaim, saying, "Oh, yes, that's just what he was like," much as we might say of a lifelike painting, "That's Fred all right. It's just as if he were speaking to us right now." You say, "But did Fred ever *really* wear such a bright blue velvet jacket? I can't say I remember ever seeing him in it, but it's just the *sort* of jacket he loved to wear. It's Fred—no mistake about that." The blue jacket might have been the artist's symbol of Fred. The Evangelist's aim was to produce a portrait much as a good portrait painter paints a picture.

What precisely the Evangelists claim for Jesus is not entirely clear. That he was invested in some way with divine power is plainly intended by all; but scholars dispute how we are to understand this. Was he, for instance, a great teacher and prophet whom God singled out for special favor, adopting him, so to speak, in a special way above all others in our human conditon? Or was he, as traditional orthodoxy has insisted, sent out of the very Being of God to encamp for a while in human flesh "for us men and for our salvation," as the Creed has it? Much technical difficulty attends phrases such as "Son of Man" and "Son of God" as they occur in the Gospels. To understand the Evangelists' intent we have to try to get inside their minds and put ourselves into the climate of thought in which they lived. Even with all the tools of modern scholarship and our increasing knowledge of the conditions of their time, the nature of their circumstances, and the influences on their thought, getting inside their minds remains difficult.

Nevertheless, they do clearly attest one thing about him: his uniqueness. However we are to interpret the various designations they give him (Messiah, Saviour, Logos, Lord), we find that they all point to that uniqueness. John's way of expressing this is to say, as he does in the dramatic prologue to his version of the Gospel, that he was the creative "Word" or "Idea" in the very Being of God who took human flesh and dwelt among us, shining as light in the darkness.

Those who wish to learn something of the technical problems connected with biblical study before they begin this book, such as the history of the text and the principles of scholarly interpretation, may care to look first at Appendix II. Others, however, may prefer to plunge into the mainstream of the book and decide later whether they wish to tackle the Appendix afterwards. For the latter I should like to make some simple observations at the outset that should much help in understanding the Gospels. Scholars call the four Gospels "canonical" because they are the ones that were eventually adopted by the early Church as the most reliable. They also classify the four Gospels as follows: Matthew, Mark, Luke are called the Synoptics; John is in a class by itself. The Gospels as we have them are by no means the oldest part of the literature we call the New Testament. Some of Paul's letters, for instance, Galatians, are much earlier, written probably less than twenty years after the death of Jesus. None of the four Gospels was written in its present form by that time.

The Synoptics were all written in their present form two or more decades later and John last of all. The comparative lateness of the Gospels is of less importance than some might suppose. Vital, however, for an understanding and appreciation of what the Evangelists were seeking to convey is a recognition of the way in which such books were conceived. Samuel Sandmel, a Jewish scholar, went so far as to call the Gospels a *midrash* or rabbinical commentary rather than a history of the life and work of Jesus.

In using this book the reader will find it convenient to have alongside a copy of the English Bible or at least the

New Testament. Any good version or translation will do. Some may prefer the King James Version. It has well-known literary merit and has inextricably woven itself into English literature in many felicitous phrases that sound familiar even to those who never read the Bible. One recalls the story of the man who was taken to see *Hamlet* and reported afterwards that he had enjoyed it, although there were too many quotations! That version, however, was made almost four centuries ago and for that and other reasons is inevitably outdated and sometimes inaccurate. So in the absence of a very strong emotional preference for that beautiful old version, the reader will usually find a greater profit from using a good modern version such as the Revised Standard or any of the lively and admirable modern translations. Those who prefer British to American usage will generally prefer the excellent New English Bible designed for them. Both that and the Jerusalem Bible, which is my own preference and generally followed in this book when biblical passages are quoted, have been made with the utmost care and by teams of eminent biblical scholars dedicated to their task.

Each of the Evangelists tells the story in his own way, one emphasizing one aspect, another a different one. At some points the accounts do not completely agree; at many points an utterance or an episode is entirely missing from one or more of the four accounts as we have them. There are technical explanations for many of the discrepancies that we find. We need not concern ourselves here with such matters. We shall construct, instead, as far as practicable, an account of the life and work of Jesus by harmonizing the four Gospels and interpreting each passage in turn, suggesting wherever occasion demands certain hidden motifs in the Ancient Wisdom with which the Evangelists were in one way or another acquainted and that may throw light on the understanding of the text. I think the use of this method will be infinitely rewarding to many readers.

I

THE EARLY YEARS

1 *John's Hymn to the Incarnate Logos*

John begins his Gospel with a magnificent prologue saturated with theosophical images and allusions. It is in effect both a hymn to the Incarnate Logos and a summary of the entire Gospel as John presents it.

The opening phrase, *en archē*, does not refer to any point in time. It does not mean "in the beginning" in the sense of "at the beginning of a period of a trillion years" or "at the beginning of the Big Bang that brought about the universe." It has no such temporal signification. It means, rather, "archetypally"; that is, it is not an historical but a metaphysical affirmation. The divine Logos exists eternally. The Logos is eternally with the divine; the Logos *is* God. The force of the affirmation can be better understood by looking for a moment at John 8.44, where the Evil One, the Devil, is said to be a murderer, a destroyer, *ap'archēs*, that is, by nature, essentially. In contrast to the cosmic power that is by its very nature evil, the Logos is by nature essentially all-good. The Logos does not merely have good qualities such as we attribute to great heroes or saints; the Logos participates in the divine essence.

How then are we to understand the term "Logos"? Literally, it means "word" and that is how English translations generally render it: "In the beginning was the Word." The Logos is the creative idea eternally in the divine mind. The term had a long history both in Jewish and Gentile thought. Heraclitus had employed it half a millenium B.C. to denote the universal reason that governs and permeates the world. The Stoics took over that notion. In later hellenistic thought it came to signify a personified power: an intermediary agent between God and the world. John makes the Logos the creative idea in the divine mind and then goes on to the affirmation that this creative idea had been embodied in the Person of Jesus Christ, through whom we can participate in a higher form of life. We appropriate this higher life through mystical union with Christ.

Philo, the great Jewish thinker in the Alexandrian tradition, connects the Logos with the opening lines of Genesis: the Logos is the creative act of God. In certain passages in the Wisdom literature the Logos had been treated almost as an objective reality (e.g., Wisdom 9.15ff) and John may have had this concept in mind, for he would have us understand that it is through the activity of the Logos that the life-principle emerges in the universe. Through the Logos all things that are have come into being. Nothing that has ever come into being has done so without the Logos. The world (*ho kosmos*) is, then, the creation of God. John is using the theosophical models of the day, but in contrast to a notion prevalent in his time he asserts that the world is not the creation of an evil deity but of the one God who is the Source of all good.

The life the Logos brings into being includes all living entities. We who know of biological evolution and can see biological life as merely an aspect of a much vaster spiritual evolution, can appreciate better than could our forefathers what John then goes on to say: human beings have reached such a point in evolution that the life the Logos gives can become for them spiritual light. The light available to human beings cannot be grasped by living beings who are still at a lower stage of development and therefore "in the dark." Darkness cannot see light, yet light shines in the darkness. According to John (John 8.12), Jesus called himself the light of the world and promised that anyone following him will have "the light of life" (*to phōs tēs zōēs*). Life, which all living beings enjoy, contains within it more than biological existence; in it is the seed of spiritual illumination. The connection between life and light that is in John's mind may be taken from a model such as is suggested in Psalm 36.9: "with you is the fountain of life, by your light we see the light." John offers us the vision of the light of the Logos shining in a dark hole: the world. The light illuminates the darkness, yet the darkness cannot overpower the light. Spiritual power and the authority it possesses lie beyond the grasp of the dark powers of worldly ambition and greed, which cannot understand, let alone master it.

From the lofty metaphysical tone of this opening passage John suddenly changes key. A man came. His name was John. The Evangelist is alluding, of course, to John the Baptist. This man, we are told, was not the light, not the Logos; but he was sent by God to be a witness to the light, to herald the coming of the light, to speak for it.

Then John changes to yet another key. The Logos is the true light through which all enlightened human beings have received their illumination. The Logos has never been absent from the world. Wherever there has been spiritual illumination, the Logos has been in action. The Logos has been coming to human beings and human beings should be capable of recognizing the light and grasping it. By and large, however, they have not done so; nevertheless, there has been a minority. The Greek pronoun used suggests a number so small as to be incalculable. Be that as it may, it is at any rate a minority. The capacity is there in all men and women, as the seed has the capacity to become a flower; yet out of a thousand seeds that are sown only one or two may germinate. The individual who does recognize the light of the Logos has spiritually germinated and is on the way to bloom. Those who have recognized the light are further described as having attained a new birth. It is not a birth in the ordinary, biological sense, arising from "the urge of the flesh"; it is not a human but a divine occurrence; yet it transforms human beings.

Then John suddenly makes the startling proclamation that is at the heart of the Gospel as he presents it: "the Word was made "flesh" (*ho logos sarx egeneto*) and lived among us. The Logos took embodiment and encamped awhile with us. John here explicitly affirms the doctrine of the Incarnation of God in Christ, which is at the heart of Christian orthodoxy. "We saw his glory," he testifies, "full of grace and truth."

The passage up to this point (John 1.1-14) is read at the end of Mass in Roman Catholic and Anglican usage and liturgically called "the Last Gospel." At the words "the Word was made flesh," priest and people kneel in acclamation of the mystery of the embodiment of God in man. According to John this is the very heart of the Gospel.

He then quotes words attributed to John the Baptist acclaiming Jesus as greater than himself: "he who comes after me ranks before me," for Christ is eternal and always creating. As Moses brought us the Torah, the Evangelist concludes, so Christ brought grace and truth. God is invisible, yet in Jesus Christ he has been seen and known. He actually dwelt among us.

This prologue, poetical in its literary structure, is like a prelude to the symphony of the Fourth Gospel. Its central theme is the progressive manifestation of the divine light, culminating in God's mysterious embodiment in the Person of Christ. It speaks the language of ancient theosophical tradition but with a distinctive accent.

All the contrasts in John's central themes are typically Gnostic: light and darkness, life and death, liberty and bondage, truth and falsehood. They represent the duality at the root of existence as we encounter it. The positive aspects are meaningless apart from their negative poles. As modern existentialists recognize and emphatically assert, such freedom as we have emerges in a backdrop of bondage to a predetermined state of affairs over which we have no control. If I cannot change my circumstances, I can nevertheless transcend them. Were there no darkness we could not identify light. John, however, gives a special meaning to these ancient antimonies. For in representing the positive aspects as issuing from the divine creativity, he bestows a special significance on all the ancient terms. To be in darkness is to shut the door against the creative act of God. To be in falsehood is not merely to be in error about something; it is to rebel against the truth, that is, the reality, of God.

2 *Luke's Preface* LUKE 1.1-4

Luke begins by alluding to the fact that many have tried their hand at narrating the events that have occurred. Claiming to have taken account of all that had happened, he has felt he ought to put what he knows in writing. He represents himself as a reporter of events.

Luke, who is generally taken to have been the companion of Paul mentioned in various New Testament letters (e.g., Colossians 4.14) and the author of the Book of Acts, addresses his Gospel to a Roman official who was presumably interested in the Christian Way and was apparently of some rank, since Luke addresses him as "Excellency". It is reasonable to assume that the author intended to show the Christian Way in a light that would appeal to the Roman aristocracy, at least to the extent of eliminating grounds for the savage persecution of Christians to which they had been already subjected under Nero.

3 *The Genealogies*

MATTHEW 1.1-17; LUKE 3.23-38

Under Roman rule the Jews enjoyed considerable toleration. They were an accepted element in the heterogeneous mix within the Empire. To show the Christian Way as rooted in the most hallowed traditions of Judaism (and no mere upstart, dangerous new cult) was therefore plainly in the interest of the Christian community. Both Matthew and Luke provide genealogies. After the Exile, the Jews had developed a strong interest in such records, especially of prominent people in the Jewish community. Such an interest is characteristic of all societies in which the family is highly prized. That is notably the case among the Jews. The two genealogies, however, are differently conceived and the one is not reconcilable with the other. In any case, if, as may be reasonably surmised, the purpose was merely polemic, an attempt to make the Christian Way look more respectable in the eyes of the Roman Establishment, the genealogies are of no special theosophical concern.

4   The Promise of the Birth of John the Baptist

LUKE 1.5-25

Zechariah was a priest belonging to the Abijah section of the Jewish priesthood. He was married to a woman, Elizabeth, a descendant of Aaron. Both were apparently exemplary in conduct and would be much respected in their community, but they were growing old and had a sorrow. They had no children, commonly taken to be a sign of divine disfavor. One day, when it was Zechariah's turn to stand alone at the altar of incense while the people were outside, the angel Gabriel appeared to him. Angels, beings on a higher plane than are we humans, were familiar to the minds of holy men such as Zechariah. They not only read of them in Scripture, especially in the Wisdom literature; they were aware, as spiritually advanced people everywhere are aware, of dimensions of being higher than ourselves and surrounding us. (See Tobit 12.15 and Enoch 20.1-8, where seven angels are mentioned by name.) At first Zechariah was afraid, but Gabriel reassured him that his prayers had been answered. His wife would bear him a son who would be indeed a great prophet. He would come "with the spirit and power of Elijah." He would live an ascetic life, preparing the people for the Lord's coming. Zechariah was to call him John. When Zechariah expressed doubt on account of his and his wife's advanced age, Gabriel told him that because of his doubt he would be silent till the day it happened. Meanwhile, the people outside wondered why Zechariah was so long in the sanctuary. When he did reappear, they found he had been stricken dumb.

The son who was eventually born to them was to be John the Baptist, who has been accounted of extraordinary importance in Christian tradition. Passages in Matthew (Matthew 11.7, 10-11, 14-15 and 17.9-13) and elsewhere strongly suggest that Jesus, in praising John the Baptist, encouraged his disciples to recognize him as having been a reincarnation of the prophet Elijah. A venerable edict of the Sanhedrin had discouraged if not forbidden acceptance of new prophets; but if Elijah had returned in John the Baptist he did not fall under that condemnation. He was then a fitting herald of the Messiah.

5   The Annunciation   Luke 1.26-38

Luke now goes on to tell of Gabriel's annunciation to Mary, a young girl betrothed to a man called Joseph. Gabriel "went in and said to her, 'Rejoice, so highly favored. The Lord is with you.' " As Mary wonders what the angel's words portend, Gabriel reassures her. "Listen! You are to conceive and bear a son, and you must name him Jesus. He will be great and will be called the Son of the Most High." Mary protests: how can she have a child, being a virgin "knowing no man" *(epei andra ou ginōskō)*. Gabriel tells her that the Holy Spirit will come upon her. Nothing is impossible for God. He tells her of Elizabeth, accounted barren, who is even then already in the sixth month of her pregnancy. Submissively, Mary declares: "I am the handmaid of the Lord, let what you have said be done to me." Then Gabriel departs.

This story is not only a favorite subject in Catholic art; it contains the passage out of which the *Ave Maria*, that most beloved of Catholic prayers, takes its origin. It presents a stumbling block to many modern critics because of the miraculous nature of the birth it seems to predict. To the hellenistic world for which Luke was writing, however, the notion that the ordinary biological processes could be set aside by the power of God for such a unique purpose would not have seemed incredible. The notion that, as Catholic tradition has strongly insisted, Jesus was miraculously born of a Virgin Mother, is not inconsistent with what we have already seen predicated of him in the prologue to the Fourth Gospel. For if the Logos, the creative idea in the divine mind, was indeed incarnate in Jesus Christ, surely he who is the very life-principle itself, without whose activity nothing has ever come into being, could be innovative in determining the mode of his own incarnation. There are indeed strong theological as well as scientific arguments against the traditional doctrine of the Virgin Birth,[1] but the possibility should not be ruled out by anyone approaching the Gospels from the vantage point of the Ancient Wisdom.

What theosophists will readily see in the story of the Annunciation is an unfolding of higher dimensions of being to us in the human condition. According to Catholic doctrine, Mary is chosen as the vehicle of the Incarnation. She is the supreme model of humility and waitingness, the disposition that makes possible the letting in of light from beyond. Her spiritual translucency, exhibited symbolically in the Rose Window at Chartres and in thousands of other such artistic representations, makes her the symbol of all spiritual openness in both women and men. She is indeed an indispensable symbol and has acquired in Catholic tradition a multifaceted symbolic function. That she functions as a symbol of femininity, of virginity, of motherhood, is obvious, carrying over into the Chris-

[1] I have considered these in my *The Nicene Creed Illumined by Modern Thought* (Grand Rapids, Michigan: William B. Eerdmans Company, 1981), Chapter VII.

tian Way these ancient symbolic functions. But she also
becomes, for example, the symbol of the whole People of
God; that is, of all who are on the way toward a higher
evolutionary stage of development. Without Mary the
whole drama of the Gospels becomes unintelligible. She
is a vital key to an understanding of its esoteric significance.

6   The Magnificat   LUKE 1.39-56

Mary then goes out to a town in the hill country of
Judaea, to Zechariah's house. There she visits Elizabeth,
who acclaims her as the most blessed of women, whereupon Mary utters the words that have become one of the
most famous canticles in the Christian liturgy: "My soul
proclaims the greatness of the Lord." It is a song in praise
of God's act in showing the emptiness of the world's
values and the victory of divine ones. He has pulled
princes down from their thrones and exalted the humble
and weak, sending the rich away empty and laying a table
for the hungry. Mary's song is saturated with allusions to
passages from the Hebrew Bible, including Hannah's song
(I Samuel 2.1-10), and is plainly designed to show the continuity of the Christian Way with the old religion. What
is being done fulfills the divine promise to come to the
help of Israel, showing God's mercy to Abraham and all
his descendants.

Those attuned to spiritual realities around them see
every day the victory of the values of those who prize
them and the futility of the pride and ambition and greed
of the world. The *Magnificat* is the hymn of every soul in
the struggle to get beyond the morass of the world into
the realm where love and light prevail.

7   The Benedictus   LUKE 1.57-80

John the Baptist is duly born. Eight days later, according to custom, he is to be circumcised and named. Also

following custom, he is about to be named Zechariah after his father, but his mother intervenes. She wants him to be called John. His father, still unable to speak, writes down the name *John* and as he does so his speech returns. In an outburst of joy he praises God in another canticle that also has deep roots in its Hebrew precursors and glows with esoteric meanings. This canticle, the *Benedictus*, outwardly celebrates the joy of the birth of the little child who is destined to become the herald of the Lord, bringing to his people "knowledge of salvation"; but it is also the song of all who have attained to the higher states of consciousness and are enabled therefore "to give light to those who live in darkness and the shadow of death." It is the song of all engaged in the struggle of working through their self-imposed karmic imprisonment to the victory of the spirit. This is indeed the whole motif of the Gospel drama.

8   *The Nativity*

MATTHEW 1.18-25, 2.1-12   LUKE 2.1-21

In both Matthew and Luke, angels are featured in the circumstances attending the birth of Jesus.

Matthew begins his account by telling of Joseph's vision in which an angel comes to him in a dream. He had been troubled on learning of Mary's pregnancy and, being an upright man, he had thought the right thing to do was to send her away privately, avoiding scandal. The angel tells him he is not to do so, for the child in Mary's womb is "by the Holy Spirit." Then Joseph awakes and does as the angel has bidden.

Luke begins by reporting the issuance of a decree of the Roman Emperor that there should be a census taken of the whole world. In obedience to the decree, Joseph set out from Nazareth to Bethlehem to be registered with Mary. While they were at Bethlehem, the time came for Mary to have the child. Finding no lodging, she wrapped him in swaddling clothes and laid him in a manger. Once again an angel comes into the picture, alerting nearby shepherds who were at first terrified at the light shining around them. Then the angel brings them the good news: a child has been born in this, the city of David, Bethlehem, and it is the Christ. He is, even now, lying in a manger. Then the voices of a great assembly of angels join in singing the *Gloria in excelsis:* "Glory to God in the highest heaven, and peace to men who enjoy his favor." Although some manuscripts would justify the common rendering "good will to men," the best have "peace to men who enjoy his favor" (*eirēnē en anthrōpois eudokias*). Significantly, the *shalom*, the salutation of peace, is for those who are already on their way to higher dimensions of being and are therefore said, in the language of the time, "to enjoy the favor of God."

Although the historical accuracy of Luke's details is questionable, there seems to be no doubt that a census was in fact taken at about the time in question, as the Jewish historian Josephus attests. Of much more theosophical importance is the symbolism Luke uses. Shepherds, unlike the lawyers and the scribes, represent lowly, down-to-earth folk. They are the ones who hear the angelic voices, for their ears are already attuned to the wonders of nature and it is but one step beyond to the voice of angels.

The shepherds go to see for themselves and, sure enough, the baby is there in the manger. They tell everybody about what they have seen and heard.

Luke's account concludes with the immensely striking statement that Mary, unlike the shepherds, did not so behave. She treasured everything she had heard and pondered it all in her heart. She had an unutterable secret. The most profound intimacies of the human soul with the divine are always inexpressible, as is attested by all the great mystics. Mary, the symbolic type of expectancy and mystical awareness of the divine power within her, is silent, serenely aware of the wonder of the unique mission she has received from God. Authenticity needs no advertisement. She has nothing to say, knowing that the divine power that has come upon her will say it far better than could she. That she had a secret to be imparted in later years to certain intimate friends, who were disciples of Jesus, is not explicitly stated by Luke, but this is very probably a hidden meaning, in view of later developments. She would then have become the focus of an esoteric circle within the apostolic group.

Luke adds to his account a mention of the circumcision of Jesus according to custom and the naming of him by the name the angel Gabriel had assigned to him. Matthew, however, adds a story of extraordinary interest to theosophists. Wise men *(magoi)*, guided by a mysterious star, come to Jerusalem "from the east" and inquire about the King of the Jews. Herod, hearing of this, calls the *magoi* and learns from them privately the exact details of the star that has guided them. He bids them go to Bethlehem and bring him back news of the child so that he, too, may come at once to worship him. The *magoi* then go to Bethlehem, still guided by the star, and find the house and Mary and the child. Falling down to worship the child, they bring out their treasures: gold, frankincense, and myrrh. Warned in a dream not to return to Herod, they leave Palestine and travel back to their own country another way.

Matthew makes no mention of their number. Origen seems to have been the first to specify three, perhaps on account of the three types of gifts that Matthew says they offered. This has come to be the general tradition and from the sixth century they have even been given names: Gaspar, Melchior, and Balthasar. The Milanese claimed to have come into possession of their relics, brought from Constantinople in the fifth century, and these, taken to Germany by Barbarossa in 1162, are now housed in Cologne Cathedral. The *magoi* were widely venerated in the Middle Ages and have been a favorite subject in Christian art. There is a painting representing them in the Priscilla Catacomb, dating from the second century.

That the Evangelists should seek to connect Jesus with the best in Jewish tradition is, for reasons already suggested, easily understood. They symbolize, of course, the first recognition by Gentiles of Jesus as the Christ. But why *magoi* from the east when any Gentile would do for that purpose? The *magoi* could be members of the Persian priestly caste, but anyone possessing occult knowledge could qualify for the title *magos*. From their preoccupation with astrology the *magoi* would seem to be practitioners of occult wisdom. They might have come from Babylonia, the home of astrology, or possibly from Arabia. The story is connected with various Old Testament texts, as is almost everything relating to the nativity of Jesus; but the introduction of *"magoi* from the east" has, to theosophists, a very special meaning. Jesus is not only the Messiah the Jews awaited; he is the Christ, the focus of all that the Ancient Wisdom is about. He makes his appearance with no public recognition in his homeland. On the contrary, he glides into the world in total obscurity, unnoticed in the midst of the crowds assembled for the census. Neither his own people nor the Romans who are administering that bureaucratic exercise could possibly have taken any notice of him. He is hidden from their eyes. But the *magoi*, as representatives of the Ancient Wisdom, find their way to him.

9   *The Nunc Dimittis*   LUKE 2.22-39

The center of the story of the visit of Mary and Joseph to the Temple, where they offer a pair of turtle-doves in sacrifice, consists in aged Simeon, who has been divinely assured that he would not die before seeing the Messiah. Simeon, represented as an upright and observant Jew, takes the child Jesus into his arms, blesses him, utters the beautiful words of the canticle now known as the *Nunc Dimittis*: "my eyes have seen the salvation which you have prepared for all the nations to see," a light for the Gentiles, the glory of Israel. He then makes a prophecy. The child is to be great. He will be a sign that is rejected. A sword is to pierce his mother's soul. All this "so that the secret thoughts of many may be laid bare." An elderly widow, Anna, a prophetess, who spent all her time in the Temple, happened to come by at this time and she, too, spoke of the child in connection with the deliverance of Jerusalem. Mary and Joseph stand in wonderment at all that is said. Then they return to their home.

10   *The Flight to Egypt*   MATTHEW 2.13-23

Yet another angel appears to Joseph, this time to warn him to take the mother and child to Egypt, because Herod is planning to kill the babe. Herod, infuriated at having been outwitted both by the wise men and by Joseph, orders the massacre of all male children under the age of two. Eventually, however, Joseph, in Egypt, is apprised in a dream of Herod's death. He returns to Israel with Mary and the child and they settle in Nazareth.

In the crypt of the ancient church of St. Sergius, in the Coptic Christian quarter of Cairo, is shown today the place where, *according to legend*, the Holy Family stayed during their sojourn in Egypt.

11   *The Hidden Years*   LUKE 2.40-52

Luke is the only one of the four Evangelists who tells us anything significant about the life of Jesus before he emerges in full manhood to pursue his ministry. From passages in Mark and Matthew (Mark 6.1-5; Matthew 13.54-58) we learn quite incidentally that Joseph was a carpenter, for when Jesus, in the course of his ministry, returns to Nazareth, his home town, the people there are unwilling to accept him because they recognize him as "the carpenter's son" and cannot see how he could have come by all the learning he professes. Where, they ask, in effect, could he have acquired it?

Some have speculated that he traveled abroad, perhaps even to India, returning to his homeland with exotic learning to which his Palestinian compatriots were unaccustomed. Such theories are unsupported by any substantial evidence either in the Gospels or elsewhere. Moreover, not only are such theories unlikely; they are unnecessary, since, as we have seen, foreign influences had affected Jewish thought for centuries before Jesus' birth. The form his ministry took, with his celibate community, would have been alien to classical Hebrew ideals and practice but would not be in itself remarkable in his time, when communities such as the Essenes had been long known.

Luke provides an additional reason for accounting such speculations as unnecessary as they are unsupported. After telling us that Jesus, as a child, grew to maturity, was filled with wisdom [*plēroumenon sophias*] and that the divine favor was with him [*charis theou ēn ep' auto*], he goes on to relate that Mary and Joseph were in the habit of going up to Jerusalem every year for the Passover. When Jesus was twelve they went as usual. On their way home they noticed he was missing and went back to look for him. After much searching they at last found him in the Temple, sitting among the doctors, listening to them and asking them questions. Those who heard him were astounded at his intelligence and his responses. Mary and Joseph chide him, telling him, as any loving parents would, how worried they had been. Jesus, in turn, asks them why they had been searching all over for him when they might have known that he would be in the Temple, "busy with my Father's affairs." Mary and Joseph, according to Luke, did not understand what he meant by this.

If by the age of twelve Jesus was able to discuss learned matters with the doctors in the Temple and astonish them with his answers (no doubt also his questions), we should not be content to ask merely, as did the townsfolk in Nazareth much later on, how he came by the learning he evinced as a rabbinical teacher. We must surely ask, rather, how he had already acquired the capacity at the age of twelve to discourse with the doctors. True, even by this early age he might have encountered a learned traveller in his home town, but that in itself could not explain the precocity and the erudition he exhibited as a boy of twelve. Those of us accustomed to theosophical ideas must surely find a simpler explanation for the kind of wisdom that Jesus constantly showed in his teaching and healing ministry. He was born with it. If, as reincarnationists know, we carry over from a previous life certain capacities learned from past experiences, surely we can have no difficulty in seeing that if Jesus, as John says, pre-existed in a very special way, he would not need to be taught in the way most men have to be taught. He already knew, already had the wisdom within him, and would need only to let it mature and to take possession of it.

Luke adds only that after this episode Jesus went down with his parents to their home in Nazareth and lived "under their authority" (ēn hypotassomenos autois), that Mary "stored up" all these things in her heart, and that Jesus increased in wisdom, in stature, and in favor with God and men. Traditionally, the period between his discoursing with the doctors in the Temple and his public emergence as a teacher and healer is about eighteen years, that is, till he was about the age of thirty. The tradition is founded on what Luke tells us (Luke 3.1-2) about the date of the appearance of John the Baptist as a prophet (the fifteenth year of the reign of Tiberias) and the baptism of Jesus at his hands, in connection with which Luke explicitly says that Jesus was about thirty at the time.

Speculations about travels Jesus might have made during these "hidden" years of his youth may be connected with a foolish and patently fabricated and malicious story that gained currency in certain circles in Europe to the effect that Jesus was the illegitimate son of Mary and a Roman soldier called Pandara or Panthera. Taken to Egypt by his stepfather, Josue ben Parania, he studied sorcery and then returned to Israel to practice his arts, which eventually led to his execution. In this scurrilous story, Mary is described as the wife of a perfumer, possibly from a confusion with Mary Magdala, since the latter name can mean "hairdresser". The name attributed in this story to the soldier, Panthera, may be due to a misunderstanding of the Greek *Parthenos*, meaning virgin, the designation so widely used of Mary by Christians. Josue ben Parania was a real person, but he died in 79 B.C. This story has all the marks of a crude fable.

Although modern biblical scholarship has shown that the Gospels do not provide us, and could not possibly have purported to provide us, with the kind of biography of Jesus we tend to expect today, the general account they present is singularly convincing in its way as far as it goes. From them and from the rest of the New Testament and other early Christian literature we do have some information out of which we can construct at least an impressionistic picture of his personality, his teaching, and his ministry of healing, with the aid of what is known from a variety of sources about life in his time and in his circumstances. Within this general framework we may cautiously speculate about details, but where we lack evidence of any kind, reverent skepticism is more spiritually profitable than wild speculation. This is especially the case when, as I have already suggested, speculation is by any reckoning unnecessary and its results unhelpful from any point of view. We do know a great deal about Jewish life, not only from the Bible but from both the Babylonian and Palestinian Talmuds, the Mishna, and other literature, and we have learned in recent decades a very great deal about Gnostic influences on early Christianity. It is to such sources that we can profitably look for an understanding of the relation of Jesus to the Ancient Wisdom.

II

THE PREPARATION

12   *The Preaching of John the Baptist*
Matthew 3.1-12   Mark 1.1-8   Luke 3.1-20

All three Synoptics give an account of the preaching of
John the Baptist, forerunner of Jesus. Mark begins his
Gospel by quoting Isaiah (Isaiah 40.3) in which the
prophet speaks of sending a messenger, a voice crying in
the wilderness: "Prepare a way for the Lord, make his
paths straight." The Baptist appears in the wilderness of
Judaea proclaiming a baptism of repentance and the forgiveness of sins. He baptized in the River Jordan, possibly
within the sight of Qumran. Some think he may have
belonged to the Qumran community and then gone out
on his own. Be that as it may, he was an ascetic, wearing
a coarse garment and living on whatever he could find in
the desert. In the course of his preaching, he spoke of
someone who was to follow him who would have far
greater spiritual power, whose sandals he was not worthy
to kneel down to tie. While John baptized people with
water, the one who was to follow him would baptize with
the Spirit of God.

23

24

He spoke harshly, telling his hearers that retribution was coming, but if they would be prepared and repent by changing their way of life, they would be ready for the Good News that was on its way. When the people asked what sort of preparation was needed, he urged them to share their goods; for instance, if a man had two tunics he should give one to another who has none. He urged the tax collectors not to collect more than the fair rate and the soldiers to be content with their pay. According to Matthew he was especially severe on the Pharisees, members of a Jewish group celebrated for strict observance of the Law, and on the Sadducees, another conservative group, in both cases for their pride and smugness in supposing that their strict outward observances would save them. This type of preaching was not entirely novel to his hearers, but apparently made such a strong impression on them that some asked whether he might be the Messiah. This he denied, insisting that nevertheless he was the herald of him who was on his way. In the course of his preaching he rebuked Herod Antipas for his manner of life, especially for his adulterous union with Herodias, the wife of Herod's half-brother Herodes. The offended Herod countered by imprisoning John in the Dead Sea fortress of Machaerus (as we learn from Josephus).

The Baptist, a strange, lone figure, must indeed have seemed to some a reincarnation of Elijah, a very great prophet in the time of Ahab in the ninth century B.C., who when in hiding near the brook Cherith, was fed by ravens (I Kings 17.2-8).

13 John Baptizes Jesus

MATTHEW 3.13-17   MARK 1.9-11   LUKE 3.21-22

Mark calls the baptism that John administered "baptism of repentance," contradistinguished from the baptism of Jesus, which was to be baptism of the Holy Spirit (Acts 11.16). The Qumran Scrolls indicated that baptism of the kind that John administered was practiced by the Qumran sect. It was symbolic only, as the Manual of Discipline (the rule of the Qumran community) makes clear. The cleansing takes place only by inward submission to God and the divine ordinances. The baptism has no value in itself; it is merely a token of inward repentance.

Jesus, in submitting to baptism by John, recognized the importance of what John was doing and of his function in the divine drama. It was in some way a turning point in Jesus' life. All three accounts of this episode are brief and all indicate that the Spirit of God came upon Jesus, accompanied by a heavenly voice saying: "You are my son, my Beloved; my favor rests on you." The Baptist comes both in the role of a deeply religious Jew and in that of a religious reformer, urging his hearers to look to the inward meaning of their ancestral religion and to see outward observances as mere tokens of that inward reality.

Jesus, in submitting to John's baptism, was aligning himself with that teaching, which is central to his own. The Gospels represent the style of life of Jesus and his disciples as different from that of John the Baptist; nevertheless, John's emphasis on inwardness prefigures that of Jesus. The trappings of religion are only the box enshrining the jewel, which is the spiritual reality. That this reality should have beautiful outward tokens may be admirable, even most desirable. The outward shell, the casket holding the jewel, may even guide people to the reality. From exoteric religion one may learn the path to the esoteric truths to which it points. But to take the outward form for the inner reality and teach others to do so can be the most pernicious kind of irreligion if, as so often happens, it halts the progress of the soul by blinding and stultifying it.

14   *The Temptation of Jesus*
MATTHEW 4.1-11   MARK 1.12-13   LUKE 4.1-13

The drama of the Temptation is set in the wilderness, whither Jesus has gone, "led by the Spirit." The agent of temptation is Satan. The story is charged with deeply theosophical significance: the powers of good and evil are ranged against each other and the combat is intensely fierce because it occurs at the highest spiritual level. Matthew's account is the most climactic.

First Satan suggests to Jesus that he use his spiritual power to turn the stones into loaves of bread. Bread is good; it is represented in the Bible as the staff of life. Jesus is hungry after a long fast. Why not use spiritual power to provide food for the body? There are echoes of the story (Exodus 16.12-35) of the manna that fell on the ground, providing food for the Israelites while they were in the desert between Egypt and Canaan. Jesus tells Satan, in effect, that there is spiritual as well as physical food and that man needs the former as much as the latter.

Then Satan leads Jesus to the pinnacle of the Temple, quoting Scripture (Psalm 91.11-12) where the Psalmist tells us of God's providing angels to guard us at every step we take. He urges Jesus to jump down, defying the law of gravity and relying on angels to bear him up. Jesus counters with another text (Deuteronomy 6.16) to the effect that one is not to put God to the test. Divine power is not something that one harnesses like electricity or water to serve one's needs whenever one chooses to press a button. We do not control it like that. We learn as we advance in spirituality to participate in it, but it is not ours to use or abuse at our pleasure like a toy.

Finally, Satan takes Jesus to a high mountain from which he can look down and see all the kingdoms of the world and the splendor of them spread before him in one great panorama. Satan, indicating that he holds sway over all the world, offers it all to Jesus on condition that Jesus recognize him, worship him, and serve him. In this last stage of the Temptation, the nature of the warfare is set forth in familiar Gnostic terms. The forces of the world are fundamentally demonic; they are in the hands of Satan. Nevertheless, Satan's power over the world is threatened by the power of God. The bitterest struggle is at the point where Satan challenges the divine power directly. If only he can enlist the divine power itself in the service of evil, he will reign supreme. The Devil's interest lies not in tempting frail, feeble characters but in seducing great, magnanimous spirits. The higher one goes in the scale of being, the more terrible the nature of the temptation to serve evil rather than good forces.

Jesus retorts by quoting the injunction in the Torah (Deuteronomy 6.13) to serve God alone. At this Satan leaves him, although according to Luke's version, only for awhile (apestē ap' autou archi kairou).

The story is full of echoes of biblical themes. According to the Torah, God led the Israelites into the wilderness and caused them to be hungry in order to test them. "Learn from this that Yahweh your God was training you as a man trains his child." (Deuteronomy 8.2-6) The story in Exodus that Moses found manna for the people in the wilderness suggests that the Jews would expect the same sort of material reward from the Messiah. They would expect an earthly kingdom with earthly rewards. Jesus, however, perceives that the Kingdom of God is not of that sort. It is a spiritual kingdom, a power to be awakened within each person who becomes an heir to it.

The standing on a pinnacle of the Temple recalls a rabbinical tradition that predicts that when the Messiah comes he will stand on the roof of the Holy Place and tell the poor that the time of their redemption is here. But Jesus renounces that kind of social revolution. His concern is for the evolution of the spiritual reality in man.

Again, in the final temptation is an echo of the promise that the future King of Israel will rule over all the nations of the earth (Psalm 2.7); but Jesus perceives that the nature of the Kingdom of God is inward. The rule must proceed from within by a raising of the level of spiritual awareness, not by a flourishing and rattling of swords. That is how the transformation of the world must begin. There is no instant cure for social and economic woes. There are no short cuts. Spirituality does not come in a cosmetic package but through radical treatment in which the gold is sifted from the dross.

The karmic law cannot be sidestepped. The spirit of man must be cleansed before it can make progress. Jesus, in the end, is to provide the supreme example of triumph through suffering. In the Temptation in the wilderness the alternatives are considered and rejected.

15 *Agnus Dei* JOHN 1.19-36

Priests and Levites ask John the Baptist who he supposes himself to be. By what right did he baptize? John, once again quoting Isaiah, says he is but a voice crying in the wilderness to prepare the way of the Lord. The following day he sees Jesus approaching and exclaims: "Behold the Lamb of God, who takes away the sin of the world!" He adds that even he, John, had not at first recognized Jesus as Messiah. Then again, the next day, John was standing with two of his disciples and as he saw Jesus walking by he again cried: "Behold the Lamb of God!"

According to a general expectation, there was to be a purification of the people before the coming of the Messiah (Ezekiel 36.25; Zechariah 13.1; Isaiah 52.15), so baptizing had a messianic significance. We are to understand that John the Baptist already knew Jesus as a friend. But only when Jesus submitted to his baptism and John saw the Spirit of God descend upon him did John grasp the situation: *this* is the Messiah. John, with clairvoyant eyes, had perceived in that moment the extraordinary character of Jesus.

John the Baptist is reported as using the remarkable title "Lamb of God." Many scholars suppose this was added by John the Evangelist writing long after the scene occurred. At any rate the symbolism is manifold. It obviously brings up the image of the sacrificial lamb of the Passover; but conjoined with it is an allusion to Jesus as the Servant of God (Isaiah 53.7). The use of the title occurs very frequently in the Apocalypse and in several senses. The lamb was a traditional symbol of innocence and moral purity.

The acclamation has become an integral part of Catholic liturgy: the *Agnus Dei* of the Mass.

16   *The First Disciples*   JOHN 1.37-51

According to the Fourth Gospel, Andrew and Simon heard John the Baptist acclaim Jesus and went at once to follow Jesus, staying with him for the rest of that day. Jesus, looking hard at Simon, told him he was to be called Cephas, an Aramaic word meaning "rock." This nickname becomes in Greek *petros.* Thus Simon became Peter or Simon Peter.

The Synoptics, as we shall see, have a somewhat different account of the connection by which these two attached themselves to Jesus, but in principle what they say broadly accords with John's version. In the Fourth Gospel they are presented as friends and followers of the Baptist, so providing a link between the Baptist's ministry and that of Jesus.

The next day Jesus met Philip, whom he told to follow him. Philip informed Nathanael that they had found Jesus of Nazareth, the one foretold in prophecy. "From Nazareth?" Nathanael cries. "Can anything good come out of there?" Apparently he, coming from the nearby village of Cana, harbored the prejudice that is so common among the inhabitants of one village towards those of a neighboring one. But the symbolism is obvious: such narrow, trivial prejudices are potent factors in hindering our spiritual progress. Philip does not get involved in an argument at that level. He simply says, "Come and see." Nathanael does go to see, and Jesus remarks, *"There* is an Israelite worthy of the name!" Nathanael asks how Jesus knew him and Jesus tells him that he had already seen him "under the fig tree" even before Philip announced him. Nathanael, impressed, acclaims him as the Son of God, as King of Israel. Jesus tells him he will see wonders far greater—even the heavens opening and angels ascending and descending above him. This start-

ling symbol, reminiscent of Jacob's ladder (Genesis
28.12), signifies the constant traffic between our dimension of being and a higher one that interpenetrates it,
although many people do not even notice.

The identity of Nathanael is not entirely clear, but
probably most scholars would identify him with Barthol-
omew. The fig trees typifies the Torah (cf. Luke 13.6ff.).

17 *The First Miracle* JOHN 2.1-11

The Hebrew language has no word for "nature" and
none for "miracle" as the term is commonly understood
as an event contrary to the laws of nature. In Hebrew a
miracle is simply a wonder or portent (*mōpēt*), a sign or
something attracting attention (*'ôt*), and *pālā*, something
that is simply extraordinary, unexpected. The New
Testament generally follows this Hebrew mold of
thought. It does not seem to have been much (if at all)
influenced by Greek conceptions of nature, which were
more philosophical. So words used in the New Testament
such as *dynamis* (power) and *sēmeion* (sign) do not con-
note the miraculous in the popular modern sense. This
is of the greatest importance in understanding the so-
called miracle stories in the Gospels. The Hebrews in
primitive times attributed thunder, lightning, earthquakes and other startling phenomena to God, not to
nature. They did not distinguish a natural and a "super-
natural" order but simply perceived that things sometimes behaved in astonishing ways, not as they behave in
our day-to-day experience. One does not see an eclipse of
the sun every day, for instance; it is fairly rare. It is
interpreted as a portent or a sign but not as an affront
to the "laws of nature," for they had no theory to make
such a concept possible.

We ought to bear this in mind when approaching any
of the miracle stories in the Gospels. Nature, as Spinoza
and others have perceived, is an aspect of divine Being.
Yet what scientists are trying to understand in their work
in physics and biology and astronomy (what we call

natural sciences) is only a part or aspect of reality. We may say, if we wish, that it is an aspect of God. That is what Kepler was saying, in effect, when, looking through his telescope, he said, "O my God, I am thinking thy thoughts after thee." But divine Being transcends what scientists properly have as their concern. We shall see how this works out as we look at the other miracles in the Gospels. Meanwhile let us look at the first that is recorded, the "turning of water into wine."

There are many explanations that do not require us to think in terms of acting "against nature," of "overruling nature." The occasion was a wedding. The household had run out of wine, or so it was said. We should bear in mind considerations such as the following. People on such occasions, especially people in relatively primitive circumstances, are easily embarrassed. Suppose, for instance, that they did have some wine, but not enough to go around another time, so that if they served it some guests would get it and others not. This could be so socially embarrassing that they might well prefer to hide the few bottles they had and simply say they were out of wine. If, however, the limited supply were to be distributed in the six stone jars that were standing empty, and these were then filled with water, there would be plenty to go round. By the time the guests at such a festive occasion had consumed the first supply they would find the diluted wine acceptable and might well account it even better.

To say, as many would, "Oh, is that all? No miracle? Just a little sleight of hand?" is to miss the whole point. To have the sensitivity to see beyond the obvious, understand the psychological situation, and so act that everybody is made happy is indeed to work wonders. Anyone who doubts that should try it. It is not easy. Of course no one can tell what exactly did happen or might have happened on any such hypothetical occasion. There is no need, however, to presuppose a turning upside down of the way nature uniformly behaves. The sign, the wonder, is far more splendid when we do not resort to any proposal such as that God sets aside his own workings in the universe to make an exception in order to provide more wine at a wedding feast. Whatever the explanation of such miracle stories is to be, it must not be anything like that. At the same time we must bear in mind that if nature is indeed an aspect of God, if as the Psalmist says (Psalm 19.1) "the heavens declare the glory of God," we shall expect the universe to yield untold wonders of which we still know little. The whole realm of parapsychology, for example, has already shown that there are indeed many phenomena that do not contravene nature but show that our common understanding of it is far too limited.

III

PUBLIC APPEARANCE

18 *Jesus Cleanses the Temple*   JOHN 2.12-26

After a brief stay at Capernaum, Jesus goes up to Jerusalem for the Passover. In the Temple he found people selling cattle and sheep and pigeons. He saw moneychangers sitting at their counters—all the familiar features of the ecclesiastical commercialization of religion. According to John, Jesus was so angry that he found some cord, made a whip out of it, and used it to drive the dealers out of the Temple. Then he upset the moneychangers' tables, scattering the coins, and cried out, "Take all this stuff away and stop turning my Father's house into a market." When asked what sign he could give to justify what he had done, he challenged his questioners to destroy "this temple" (*ton naon*) and in three days he would rebuild it. The Jews reminded Jesus that the Temple had taken forty-six years to build, yet he proposed to rebuild it in three days!

John's interpretation of what Jesus meant is of much theosophical interest. To suppose, as did his hearers,

34

that Jesus was speaking of the Temple out of which he had just thrown the traders and moneychangers was surely a reasonable interpretation of his words. John asserts, however, that he was in fact speaking about his body, not the stones of the Temple. The word *naos* (temple) does indeed have a figurative sense: the place where the divine power dwells. The divine power dwelt indeed in his body, which they could destroy, but he would raise it up in three days. John tells us that the disciples never understood what he meant till after the resurrection. If such a seemingly straightforward utterance of Jesus could have such hidden meaning, how much esoteric significance is likely to lie behind everything in his recorded sayings!

The concluding sentences in this passage speak quite openly of the clairvoyant powers of Jesus. Many, during his stay for the Passover, professed belief in his claims as they understood them, but Jesus "did not trust himself to them." Why? He apparently saw through them. He never needed anybody to recommend people to him, nor did he stand in any danger of being influenced by gossip. "He could tell what a man had in him," says John. Such perception of character is one of the many gifts with which deeply spiritual people are endowed and Jesus by all accounts had it *par excellence*. We have already noticed his spontaneous appraisal of Nathanael. The ability is made possible through awareness of dimensions of reality beyond mere physical shape and size and texture. It is one of the more immediate rewards of a spiriual life.

All the Synoptists relate the same story but place it after the final entry of Jesus into Jerusalem. See Section 118.

19 *Rebirth, Baptism, and Nicodemus*
JOHN 2.25-3.24

While Jesus was in Jerusalem for the Passover he met a distinguished Pharisee, Nicodemus, who came to see him by night and indicated that he regarded him as a divinely approved teacher. Only someone who was authentic could do the sort of things he was doing. When Jesus told Nicodemus that no one can "enter into the Kingdom of Heaven" unless he be reborn, Nicodemus asks, "How so? Go back into his mother's womb and be reborn?" Jesus explains that he must be reborn "of water and the Spirit," because what is born physically is one thing; what is born in the realm of the Spirit is another. He goes on to say that spiritual people are like the wind. "Spirit" and "wind, breath" are the same word in Hebrew (*ruach*) and Greek (*pneuma*), so there is a sort of pun in what Jesus says: the wind blows where it pleases. You hear it, but you can't tell whence it came or whither it goes. So it is, he says, with spiritual people. So far as the physical man goes you can tell when he was born and when he died; but spiritually awakened people have a long history and a great destiny far beyond the record of their life from birth to death. Nicodemus is still puzzled. Jesus chides him. What he has been talking about is such an elementary question in the Ancient Wisdom, a matter everybody with any pretentions to religious leadership should know about. (Yet how few religious leaders have penetrated even that much into the spiritual realities around them!) If Nicodemus is not even at this level, how will he ever understand the mysteries Jesus is to reveal? We speak, Jesus told him, "about what we *know*."

John then goes on to the much-quoted words he attributed to Jesus: God loves the world so much that he gives his only Son, so that everyone who believes in him may not be lost but may have eternal life. Yet, Jesus continues, although light has come into the world, people show they prefer darkness. Why? Because they are the children of darkness. Those who do dark deeds naturally do not like the light, but those who are open to the truth love it.

Jesus makes plain that he is not the kind of teacher who has to rely on manipulating texts and commentaries. He is not talking from hearsay. He is talking about what he knows, what he has actually perceived in the realm of the Spirit. People who are afraid to enter the realm or even look at it will obviously be unable to understand even the most elementary facts about it, any more than a tone-deaf person would be expected to understand about octaves and diminished fifths, about sharps and flats. He might be able, through a study of the grammar of music, to identify such things on a musical score, but he has never experienced them and so really does not know what you are talking about.

Then Jesus goes into the Judaean countryside. Both he (or his disciples) and John the Baptist engage in administering their respective baptisms. Some of John's disciples get into an argument with a Jew about the religious concept of purification. They ask John the Baptist about the fact that Jesus is baptizing too, noting that "everyone is going to him." John replies that Jesus will grow greater and he, John, less. For John is not the Christ but only his herald.

20 Jesus Departs for Galilee
MATTHEW 4.12   MARK 1.14   JOHN 4.1-3

It was about this time that John the Baptist was arrested. Everyone knew that Jesus and his disciples were also baptizing. Trouble was brewing. Jesus resolved, therefore, to leave the area and go north through Samaria to his homeland, Galilee.

21 The Samaritan Woman at the Well
JOHN 4.14-42

The Samaritans lived a separate life from the Jews. They accepted only the Torah and had built a temple on Mount Gerizim. Although this temple had been destroyed in 128 B.C., the site remained a place of worship and pilgrimage for the Samaritans in the time of Jesus. The Samaritan community has continued down to the present day, although now attenuated to a few hundred people.

Jesus, who had to pass through Samaria on his way
north to Galilee, sat down at noon by the well of Jacob
at Sychar, tired after the long journey. His disciples had
gone into the town to buy food. While he was sitting
alone, a Samaritan woman came to draw water from the
well. Jesus asked her to give him a drink of water. Since
Jews did not associate with Samaritans, the woman was
astonished and said so. Jesus tells her that if only she
knew to whom she was speaking she would have been the
one to ask for water. He would have given her living
water (hydōr zōn). The woman replies with a down-to-
earth observation: "Sir, you have no bucket! How could
you get water?" The Evangelists, not least the writer of
the Fourth Gospel, love to put literalistic utterances
alongside hints at esoteric interpretations. Jesus explains
that the water he is talking about is different. The water
people draw from wells is such that, after people have
drunk it, in time they get thirsty again. By contrast, the
water he is talking about is such that once you have
drunk it, not only are you never thirsty again, the water
inside you turns into a spring that wells up providing you
with eternal life. The woman, fascinated by this notion,
asks him to give her some of this water, for then not
only would she never be thirsty, she would never need
to come to the well to draw water.

At this Jesus tells her to call her husband and come
back with him. She says she has no husband. Jesus tells
her she is indeed right in saying that she has no husband,
for she has had five and the man she now has is not her
husband. The woman, amazed, remarks that he seems to
be a prophet. She also observes that he, as a Jew, would
worship at Jerusalem, but the Samaritans at Gerizim.
To this Jesus replies that the time is coming when true
worshipers would "worship in spirit and truth," rather
than associating worship with a particular place. The
woman listens but obviously does not grasp his meaning.
She says she knows the Messiah is coming and will tell
them everything when he does. Then Jesus makes the
startling announcement, "I am he." The meaning of this

affirmation is obscure. In Greek it is simply: *egō eimi*, I am. The Hebrew counterpart, however, *ani hu* or *ani huah* (Aramaic, *ana hu*) is a ritual formula, a theophany or a summary of God's self-revelatory declarations in the ritual of the Jewish Feast of Tabernacles, having its textual focus in Isaiah 40.

What is now known from the discoveries at Qumran sheds interesting light on this. The Manual of Discipline used by the desert sect which most scholars identify as the Essenes, respects the ancient Jewish taboo against uttering the divine name (Yahweh) by substituting for it in writing four dots or the letter Aleph (A); but sometimes a circumlocution meaning "the Eternal" (a favorite in French translations, by the way) was used and also the word *huah*, an emphatic form of "he". So in the Manual of Discipline (8, 13 f.) we read that "they are to be kept apart and go into the wilderness to prepare the way of the *huah* there," presumably a compound of *huah* (he) and A, standing for God. The Qumran sect attached much importance to the Book of Isaiah, from which John the Baptist so habitually quotes and which figures much elsewhere in New Testament quotation.

Jesus, as a Jew, would never openly claim to be God. That, in Semitic tradition, is the ultimate blasphemy. Yet, by using the theophanic *ani hu*, he is saying, in effect: "Where I am, God is alive and revealing himself."

The disciples at this point return and are surprised at his speaking to a Samaritan woman. They say nothing, but instead urge him to eat. Meanwhile the woman, having put down her water jar, rushes back to the town to tell friends that she has been talking to a strange man who knows everything about her. Could he be the Messiah? While people are coming to see Jesus, he declines food the disciples have to offer, saying that he has food such as they know nothing about.

On the strength of the woman's story, many of the people who came believed Jesus might be the Messiah. After they had talked with him, some said they no longer believed only because of what she had told them; now they *knew*. Jesus stayed with the Samaritans for two days, then left for Galilee.

IV

RETURN TO GALILEE

22 *Jesus Begins Preaching in his Homeland*

MATTHEW 4.12-17   14.3-5

MARK 1.14-15   6.17-18

LUKE 3.19-20   4.14-15   JOHN 4.43-45

When Jesus heard that John the Baptist had been im-
prisoned, he began preaching to the effect that this was
the signal. The time had now come for him to call for
repentance and to preach the good news. He was already
saying that a prophet is not without honor save in his
own country. But by now people had heard of, and some
of them had seen, what he had been doing at Jerusalem
and, according to Luke, they were all impressed when he
came into the synagogue and taught.

The core of his teaching at the outset was summed up
in the announcement that "the kingdom of God is at
hand." (Matthew alone uses the phrase "the kingdom of
heaven.") It is not to be won by the political and military
means by which earthly kingdoms are won. Why? Because it is "within you" (Luke 17.21). Look inside you
and there it is! In Tennyson's words: "Closer is He than

40

breathing, and nearer than hands and feet.'' The spiritual
world is so near that you have only to turn your eyes and
ears inward and you will find it there, ready to be developed in all its beauty and glory.

Whatever the realm of the spirit is, it is not to be found
in the external physical world. Externals may aid it, as
good gardening may promote a garden's growth; but spiritual life lies inside us, as life lies inside the flowers and
the shrubs in the garden. ''Turn inwards'' is therefore the
first injunction that Jesus gives. The work of the community (the Church or whatever it be called) is of value
only to the extent that it promotes interior growth in the
individual. If it does not have this effect it is inauthentic
and has therefore no function, at any rate none of the sort
to which it pretends.

23 Jesus Cures a Dying Son

JOHN 4.46-54

A court official went to see Jesus at Cana to ask him
to come to Capernaum, where his son was dying of fever,
and cure him. He begged Jesus, ''Come before my boy
dies.'' Jesus, instead of going to Capernaum with the
man, told him he must believe. Without faith, no wonders can be done. With faith, everything is possible. Jesus
then simply told the official that his son was all right, as
he would find if he went home. When the distraught
father heard this, he believed Jesus and returned to Capernaum. Servants came out to meet him with the glad news
that the boy was all right. Asked when precisely the boy
had taken a turn for the better, they replied that the fever
had left him ''at the seventh hour.'' That was exactly
when Jesus had assured the father that all would be well
if only he believed. The whole household accepted the
cure of the boy as a sign that Jesus was no ordinary rabbinical teacher.

This is one of several stories of cures effected by Jesus
at a distance from the patient. There was no ''laying on
of hands,'' not even a word addressed directly to the boy

in his physical presence. Old-fashioned exegetes used to puzzle over how such miracles should be interpreted. Today, what we know of telepathy and other such phenomena indicates that distance is not fundamentally important in the process of spiritual healing. The clearsightedness of Jesus enabled him to sum up the whole situation. He then transferred the power he had aroused in the mind of the anxious father to the bedside of his son. An executive does not have to go to the scene to effect the result he desires; he sends out an order. So Jesus put in motion the spiritual agencies at his command. In some degree we all have such healing power. Jesus had it in a preeminent degree.

24 In the Synagogue at Nazareth
MATTHEW 4.13-16   LUKE 4.16-31

Jesus, having returned to his home town of Nazareth, went into the synagogue. He stood up, as was his custom, to read. The reconstruction of the scene is of some importance. At that time in human history the book as we know it had not been invented. Scrolls were used and were much more awkward to handle, being more like a roll of wallpaper than the book you are now reading. Moreover, a book of the Bible was not divided into chapters and verses as Bibles are nowadays. These handy divisions were a very much later invention. Finding your place was not as easy a matter as it is for us today, when any intelligent child can look up chapter and verse of a given book of the Bible. Much knowledge of the text was demanded in order to find your place in such a scroll. All this shows that Jesus was thoroughly versed in the Hebrew Scriptures. The presiding officer of the synagogue would extend the courtesy to Jesus, as a visiting rabbi, after the Torah passage (prescribed by a lectionary) had been read in Hebrew and then translated, verse by verse, into Aramaic. The passage from the Prophets may have been selected by a similar method or may have been at the choice of Jesus, but in either case skill would be required to find the place.

Jesus begins, at any rate, with a passage from Isaiah 61.1-2:

The spirit of the Lord has been given to me
for he has anointed me.
He has sent me to bring good news to the poor,
to bind up hearts that are broken;

to proclaim liberty to captives,
freedom to those in prison;
to proclaim a year of favor from the Lord,
a day of vengeance from our God.

Here was a clear announcement of the mission of Jesus as he wished it to be perceived. He has the secret of salvation and he is going to impart it to others. The "poor," as so often elsewhere in his teaching, are those who are *spiritually* impoverished. They are by no means necessarily those who happen to be economically poor. They are all whose inner life is starved or stunted. Likewise the captives are not necessarily in physical chains; they are all who are bound by spiritual bonds, enslaved to their passions or to superstition or fear, victims of their own karma. Jesus promises help for all who need it.

Handing the scroll back to the attendant, he begins to give his commentary on the passage he has read. Today, he says, the prophecy is being fulfilled. As he went on with his preaching, the people were delighted by the graciousness of his words. "Isn't this Joseph's son?" they murmured. Jesus, perceiving that they had a mind to test his reputed healing powers, said, "No doubt you are ready to quote the old proverb at me: 'Physician, heal thyself!' You will demand that I do the wonders here that you have heard I did in Capernaum. But I am telling you that a prophet is never welcome in his home town!" Then he went on to remind his hearers that Elijah and Elisha did not fare well among their own people but performed their wonders elsewhere. The obvious inference was that his hearers were too prejudiced against him in their minds to permit of his doing the wonders they expected of him.

Spiritual healing, like other wonders of the spiritual realm, cannot be ordered as one orders potatoes from the village store. It is not a service to be hired like the services of an attorney or real estate broker. Like love itself, it cannot be bought or commandeered.

Characteristically, his hearers were furious, not least since they had already been attracted to the notion of having a prophet among them who had a reputation for doing wonders. He was now declining to do so on their terms. Of course Jesus was bound to decline. Without the right disposition on the part of the recipient, even God cannot heal. The hearers, in their anger, propose to throw Jesus from a cliff, but he escapes from them, perhaps taking advantage of a moment when their fury was at its height so that they did not notice him, or perhaps by reason of the awe they felt in his charismatic presence. At any rate, he left and went to Capernaum.

25   Fishers of Men
MATTHEW 4.18-22   MARK 1.16-20
LUKE 5.1-11

The three Synoptists all refer to an incident which occurred after Jesus had left his home town and come to Capernaum on the sea of Galilee. He summoned disciples from their work as fishermen and told them that he would give them something better to do; he would make them "fishers of men." Luke, however, tells of Jesus teaching the disciples out of a boat and then telling Simon to put the boat out to sea with the object of getting a catch of fish. Simon replies that they have been working all night and have caught nothing, but that, since Jesus had asked, he would pull out and let down the nets. Then the catch is so enormous that the boat, overloaded, seems about to sink. Simon, astonished and afraid, begs Jesus to go, for he is not worthy of so holy a teacher. It is then, according to Luke, that Jesus tells Simon that he is going to make him a fisher of men.

The notion of "catching men" implies that people are there in great numbers, ready for spiritual growth. (As he puts it elsewhere in another metaphor, "the harvest is white.") But we must go out to find them. They may appear in the most unexpected places and at the most unexpected times.

26 Wonderful Cures

MATTHEW 4.23   8.1-4   14-17
MARK 1.21-45   LUKE 4.31-44   5.12-16

In Capernaum Jesus is once again teaching in the synagogue, and we are told that the people are astonished at his style. Unlike the scribes, he teaches "with authority (exousia)." In the synagogue was a man apparently deranged in mind. According to the testimony of the Evangelists, he had "the spirit of an unclean demon" (pneuma daimoniou akathartou) in him. Jesus, recognizing the power of evil spiritual agencies, challenges the evil spirit in the man, who had been shouting abusive language at Jesus. To the astonishment of the bystanders, when Jesus commands the evil spirit to shut up and come out of the man, the man's sanity returns. What sort of power has this Jesus, the people ask, to be able to order evil spirits about?

The same day he found Simon Peter's mother-in-law in bed with fever and "stood over her" and took her by the hand, whereupon she got up and was able to go about her duties in the house. The same evening people brought him others afflicted in various ways, including those deranged in mind, and he cured many of them with a word.

He went all over Galilee engaging in this healing ministry, teaching as he healed. A leper, for example, was convinced that Jesus could cure him of his dread disease. Jesus touched him and no sign of leprosy remained. Jesus told the leper to say nothing about it but to go to the priest and make the appointed offering according to Mosaic law, "as evidence for them." Stories of his wonder-working spread rapidly and many people came seeking to be cured; but Jesus then retreated for a while to the deserts where he engaged in prayer.

Anyone with any knowledge and experience of spiritual healing will understand what was going on. Jesus had in a superlative degree the power to heal the minds and bodies of men and women by drawing upon the storehouse of goodness within him, which he used to show people the nature and power of spiritual realities. The healing was a practical demonstration of the truth of what he was teaching. From this we can see well enough what kind of teaching it was: it was an awakening in his hearers of the realities of the spiritual realm about them. This was very different from the traditional kind of religious instruction to which they were accustomed. People's minds and hearts were prepared for it; nevertheless it came as a shock to them to find it done by a teacher within the rabbinic tradition and apparently faithful to the observances required by the Mosaic law. As Bergson has said, conventional religion is a derivative perversion of a once-living reality. Religious observance can lead people away from spiritual realities rather than towards them and when (as so often) it does so, it has become an impediment, not an aid, to spiritual progress.

27 The Paralytic

MATTHEW 9.1-8 MARK 2.1-12
LUKE 5.17-26

When Jesus, having returned from his meditation in the desert, was known to be available again, people brought him a man suffering from paralysis. Full of healing power, Jesus told the man that his sins were forgiven. There were a good many scribes and Pharisees around and they were shocked by Jesus' apparent claim to forgive sins, which, they murmured, belonged to God. To make such a claim was blasphemy. Jesus, aware of what they were murmuring, asked them which was easier to say: "your sins are forgiven" or "get up and walk"? Then he told the paralytic to get up, take his stretcher with him, and walk home.

The connection between the teaching of Jesus and his healing skill is strikingly brought out here. When we say that our sins are forgiven, we say that impediments to our taking hold of the spiritual realities and possession of our place in the spiritual realm are now removed by the power of love. This love is the precondition of healing. The human soul, which exercises an enormous effect on the physical body, cannot be healed until the way is prepared by the infusion of divine love. Jesus was well aware that the ultimate origin of physical disease is in the soul. To make the soul right is the most radical kind of medical treatment that can be administered.

28 *Eating Among Sinners*

MATTHEW 9.9-13   MARK 2.13-17
LUKE 5.27-32

Jesus, having called Matthew to follow him as one of his disciples, is dining at his house with some tax-collectors and sinners. Scribes and Pharisees, seizing on this fact, ask the disciples why they and their Master eat with such people. One is judged by the company one keeps.

Those who observed the ordinances of the Law chose carefully those with whom they ate. A point of legalism was obtruding in such a way as to obscure the spirituality of the message of Jesus. Jesus, having heard the complaint, replied skillfully by pointing out that he had no work to do among healthy people but only among those that needed help. His mission was not to righteous people but to sinners.

Sinners needed Jesus, he was saying, and can therefore understand and profit from his ministry. For, in the spiritual realm, love overcomes all obstacles and sinners have the capacity for loving gratitude that the smugly proud,

in their lovelessness, cannot experience and therefore
cannot show.

29 *Fasting*   MATTHEW 9.14-17   MARK 2.18-22
                                              LUKE 5.33-39

We have already seen that Jesus engaged in fasting. Yet
he and his disciples apparently did not observe all the fast
days recognized by the Pharisees. The Torah did not
demand observance of these fast days. Only one day in
the year was required by Law, namely, the Day of Atone-
ment. The Pharisees, however, had introduced a number
of fast days—for example, Mondays and Thursdays during
special seasons of prayer. The disciples of Jesus wondered
why their Master did not require the fasts prescribed by
the Pharisees, especially since John the Baptist made his
disciples fast so much.

Parables are introduced in defense of the attitude of
Jesus. One is that one does not try to mend an old garment with new cloth, for the new will only tear apart
from the old. So the new way that Jesus is preaching,
although it does not seek to separate itself from its Jewish
background, ushers in a new kind of religious liberty.
That does not mean that the disciples of Jesus are aban-
doning religious austerity and asceticism; it does mean
that they are seeking such disciplines as no more than
aids to the development of the interior life. As mere observances they are worthless in themselves. So when they
are prescribed by Pharisaic or other legislation or enact-
ment they are by no means indispensable. They are mere
methodologies, like a particular kind of bookkeeping or a
particular style of teaching. John's disciples chose a
rigorous habit of fasting, but Jesus does not attach fundamental importance to anything of this sort.

Another parable is suggested: nobody pours new wine
into old wineskins, for it will burst them. Luke has a
variant: nobody wants new wine after drinking old.

The general notion to which these parables seem to point is the incompatibility of two different ways of life. Jesus does not decry the practices of either John the Baptist or the Pharisees in respect to fasting. Nevertheless, his way of life cannot be expected to mix at all points with either the Baptist's or the Pharisees'.

Jesus is saying here very much the same as is said by many expositors of the Ancient Wisdom. No way is wrong if it leads to good spiritual results. It is much the same with the care and development of the body. If a walk after breakfast does you more good than one after dinner, by all means take it, but do not impose it on me, for I happen to prefer the opposite. Moreover, your practice fits your total way of life; it would not fit mine. What matters is the result, not the method. If Jesus taught anything, he taught individual liberty and the individual responsibility that must accompany it.

30 *The Sabbath Was Made for Man*
MATTHEW 12.1-14   MARK 2.23-28   3.1-6
LUKE 6.1-11   JOHN 5

Various doings of Jesus are linked to the general theme that the Sabbath, salutary institution though it be, is designed in the Torah only for the benefit of our spiritual development. We are not designed for upholding the institution of the Sabbath as having an intrinsic value in itself apart from us. Jesus does not in any way repudiate the value of the Law; but he insists on seeing it as an instrument to be used for spiritual attainment. The Law is not an end in itself.

The Sabbath was (and among orthodox Jews still is) very strictly observed. Although certain exceptions were made to the general rule that no work of any kind might be done on the Sabbath (for instance, to save a life), Jesus was not necessarily claiming to invoke any such legally recognized exception.

In John's story, Jesus cured a man who was unable to get into the pool at Bethesda because he had nobody to

help him and he could not walk. Jesus exercised his healing power on him and told him to take up his mat and
walk away. According to the strict interpretation of the
Torah, this was Sabbath-breaking, a sin against one of the
Ten Commandments of Moses. That Jesus habitually
ignored the strict interpretation is suggested by the use
of the imperfect tense. Apparently, moreover, the Pharisees were especially affronted by this practice. They frequently used it as evidence against him. Yet Jesus was
willing to ignore the strict letter of the Law in such a
matter and so allowed his disciples, being hungry, to
pick ears of corn as they went along their way. He reminded the objectors of the example of David, who had
eaten even the loaves of offering in the very house of God
itself, merely because he was hungry, and had given some
of it to his companions. Similarly, Jesus reminded those
who objected to his healing acts on the Sabbath that
nobody would let a sheep lie in a pit on the Sabbath; of
course one would rescue it. Is not a man more valuable
than a sheep? Surely it is better to do something to save
a life than to let life be diminished or destroyed.

This aspect of the teaching of Jesus accords strikingly
with ancient theosophical teaching. The karmic principle
is indeed a moral law of the universe, as the so-called
"laws of physics" are the "laws of nature." Moral laws
cannot be expressed in terms of a series of rules. Such
rules may be indeed most useful as guidelines. By following them, one may learn such insight into the underlying moral law that one may with the Psalmist praise
the Torah, saying "The law of the Lord is perfect, con-
verting the soul." It is perfect, however, only insofar as
it does "convert the soul." The moral law is far more
fundamental, far more inexorable, far more awesome,
than any code of ethics or list of commandments could
possibly express. Recognition of this was not new with
Jesus who was indeed saying much the same as had been
expressed in the Torah itself (Deuteronomy 6.5 and
Leviticus 19.18), which teaching is summed up by Jesus
(e.g., Luke 10.27): "You must love the Lord your God...
and your neighbor as yourself."

50

31   The Fame of Jesus Spreads
MATTHEW 4.23-25   12.15-21
MARK 3.7-12   LUKE 6.17-19

The Evangelists tell us that the repute of Jesus was growing so much that people were coming from far and wide to see him and to be cured of their ills. They were coming from Idumaea in the south and from Tyre and other cities in the north, bringing to him people who were suffering from all sorts of diseases and other afflictions. Such were the crowds that, according to Mark, Jesus asked his disciples to get a little boat so that the crowds would not press in on him too much. Jesus seems often to have used a boat from which to teach.

Luke tells us that "power came forth from him" and cured the afflicted people of their ills. Here is a clear recognition of the character of the healing. It was accomplished by the energy (*dynamis*) within Jesus, which flowed from him toward the sufferers. Both Mark and Matthew mention also that Jesus warned the people "not to make him known." The kind of psychic energy that Jesus had and used requires a special kind of concentration. When it is publicized and the subject of idle gossip and rumor, the psychic circumstances may become so altered as to diminish its healing efficacy. Everybody wanted to touch Jesus, Luke tells us, because they knew there was something infinitely beneficial flowing from him. This belief plainly stemmed from a popular awareness of the reality of the spiritual dimension and of its tremendous power for good or evil. In Jesus they perceived its healing efficacy. Jesus himself no less plainly recognized the nature of the power, which came from the divine source that was in him and that he could not allow to be idly dissipated. It must be carefully used, not scattered to the winds.

In the passage that Matthew quotes (Isaiah 42.1-4) we are confronted with the notion of the silent action of the healing power. Jesus is identified with the "servant" in the prophet's poem, who "will not brawl or shout, nor will anyone hear his voice in the streets.'' He is not a demagogue screaming to be heard and seeking publicity by every means he can contrive. On the contrary, he comes silently, noiselessly. As in Phillips Brooks's hymn:

> How silently, how silently,
> The wondrous gift is given.

Divine power needs no advertisement. Moreover, spiritual action is in the nature of the case esoteric, hidden from public view. It flows from giver to receiver as noiselessly as light beams forth. So Jesus urges his hearers not to make him known, not to spread news of his healing power, for there is no need since its results will speak for themselves. Charlatans and the like are constantly seeking publicity and, in our own time, will often hire expensive specialists in the art of attracting it. But a person endowed with authentic healing power certainly needs no such advertisement, having within him the divinely charged interior magnet that draws to him those who stand in need of healing.

32   *The Twelve Disciples*
Matthew 10.2-4   Mark 3.13-19   Luke 6.12-16

Both Mark and Luke, before listing the names of the twelve that Jesus selects out of the disciples who have gathered about him, allude to his going up into a mountain to pray. Luke says he continued in prayer all night long before making the selection. Prayer, so much misunderstood in popular forms of religion, is of immense importance, the most powerful form of energy that one can generate. It is an incalculably great force in linking ourselves to the inexhaustible source of all things, apart from whom we are spiritually bankrupt. In connection with all the great episodes recorded of Christ we find him in a remote mountainside or quiet garden, engaged in prayer.

V

THE SERMON ON THE MOUNT

33 *The Beatitudes*
MATTHEW 5.1-12   LUKE 6.20-23

The Beatitudes are a celebration of the joy of life in the spiritual dimension of existence. They spell out these joys in terms of "rewards" to come; but the joys are already present, as we shall see. The Beatitudes are so called from the Latin word "beati" used in Latin versions of the Bible and traditionally rendered "blessed" in English ones. The Jerusalem Bible and other modern translations use the word "happy," which brings out more vividly the Aramaic expression behind the words, which would be literally rendered: "O the good fortune of . . . " Luke puts the Beatitudes in the form of a direct address to the hearers. Remembering that the New Testament writers habitually use everyday Greek (neither elegant classical style nor cheap slang), we might even say, "You lucky people!"

All the beatitudes describe the spiritual reality behind the physical appearance. Here is a person who outwardly seems poor, dejected, worthless, just one in the crowd slipping by unnoticed. Inwardly, however, he or she is radiantly beautiful, already in possession of the "kingdom of heaven." Only those who are already in that spiritual dimension can recognize the radiance and the beauty, beside which the fashionable and expensive dress and rich jewels of the prosperous are but trash. Those who are in that "kingdom of heaven" are conquering the world by their interior humility, bending like the tree that yields under the weight of the snow and so, being pliable, does not break but is able to spring back again as soon as the snow melts. Adversity increases our capacity for sympathy and our receptivity to spiritual truths.

Here is someone who appears outwardly dreary and sad, not joining easily in the loud amusements of the crowd. Through his sorrow and loneliness, however, he finds his way to the hidden realm of the spirit and all its interior joys that the empty-headed extroverts know nothing about. Through the anguish of bereavement and loss, the spirit can be strengthened, achieving the interior independence and awareness that a holy solitariness can bring, causing him, as we might say, to laugh all the way to heaven.

The meek (*hoi praeis*), we are told, are to inherit the earth. Wyclif, in his medieval translation, called them "the mylde men." All the ancient sages agree that the world is not conquered by arrogance and brute force but may be won by kindness and gentility. We can see the principle at work today even in the notion of defensive driving. We win by yielding, not by aggression. Yielding is not a negative attitude; it is more positive than aggression.

Those who truly long for holiness, for purity of life, for justice, are inwardly transformed even in the anguish of their longing. Hunger and thirst for the right makes them healthy inside, and out of that interior health grows an inexpressibly joyful satisfaction, an awareness of the goodness of God that the outwardly unconcerned know nothing about.

The merciful are promised mercy. Already, through their attitude of mercy and love, they know how to appreciate such blessings.

Purity of heart is unique among the dispositions set forth in the Beatitudes. Only those who keep something of the simplicity and purity of heart that is in a little child (despite all the tribulations of life and the complexities that turn and twist our souls in the course of our pilgrimage) can hope to see divine reality at the heart of all things. In others it is so obscured that they can catch at best only a distorted glance, as through opaque glass. The complex cannot lay hold of the simple. As life surrounds us with its complexities we lose the capacity to see what really matters, so we lose out in the worst way. The "heavenly vision" is the most priceless treasure we have—all that matters in the last resort. Riches and power do not teach us anything of eternal importance; poverty and powerlessness can.

Warmongers of every kind bring only misery in their train: a trail of destruction and death. By contrast, those who are in any way ambassadors of peace, even when they are unsuccessful in their mission, create an ambience of love whose fruits grow in themselves, winning for them an interior peace that surpasses any satisfactions that the world has to offer.

Those who are engaged in so tending their souls that such spiritual vitality is awakened within them are likely, for one reason or another, to be persecuted. They are likely to arouse hostility, envy, jealousy, and fear. Prophets are in principle unwelcome guests. Men and women who exhibit the qualities celebrated in the Beatitudes become spiritual power-houses. As such they offend those to whom their spiritual attainments come as a reproach. So they may be said to invite reprisal. Others think to rob them of their treasure by bringing them down to their own pedestrian level. All this is persecution of one kind or another. Jesus reminds us that in persecution we are not alone. Never was there a prophet or wise man who was not in some way persecuted. Envy is an extremely powerful passion. It seeks to destroy. Its dog-in-the-manger attitude seeks to form a road block against positivity and progress. When one perceives such hostility one should rejoice. If the reason for it is that we have grown to such spiritual maturity as to invite such resentment, then we are indeed fortunate. The hostility has told us that we are spiritually richer than we may have supposed, since we evoke so much bitterness and envy. That is not to say, of course, that we are to wallow smugly in our consciousness of spiritual wealth. That would be to act like the miser who runs his bag of gold coins through his fingers, putting them to no better use. Our rejoicing is not to be of that kind but, rather, an encouragement to the further development of our inward treasure, the interior life whence all that is worth our while in us springs up and sends its goodness all around us, healing all that it touches.

In Luke's version, the Beatitudes are followed by a series of "Woes." The Greek (ouai) means: "distress is coming to you." It is pronounced upon the rich, because "they have their consolation." As we might say, their wealth is all they have. Apart from it they have nothing and when they leave this life they will be utterly empty. Moreover, they have no spiritual treasure within them now and so are like gilded caskets with nothing inside. Those who are content to be well fed must take warning, for while their bodies are filled with rich food, they are spiritually starving. So, too, with those laughing loudly and idly while inside they cannot even smile. How little they have to laugh about! Finally, when people are flattering you and patting you on the back, beware! They did that to the false prophets. To luxuriate in the praise of sycophants is the way to perdition; indeed, if we are titillated by them we have already lost the way.

Yet although the Beatitudes and Woes describe the actual interior states that belong to people whose outward state seems very different, they also describe a destiny. In the language of the Ancient Wisdom, the karmic principle is at work in them as everywhere else.

Those who are called blessed or happy (*makarioi*) will
reap the reward of their outlook and way of life, for they
are building up treasures for themselves for the future
that will positively and beneficially affect their whole
destiny. The others are building up "bad karma" and will
reap the fruits of what they are now sowing in and for
themselves. This karmic principle, implied no less
clearly elsewhere in the Gospels, as we shall see, is a
fundamental principle of the Ancient Wisdom, which the
Beatitudes dramatically express.

34 *Let Your Light Shine*

Jesus tells his hearers that they are "the salt of the
earth"; that is, it is they who give the earth such goodness as it has. Suppose, however, that a follower of the
Christian Way loses that goodness that has begun to grow
in him: what good is he? None. Spiritual attainment,
when it is stunted, gives place to emptiness. The soul
becomes a ruin.

Jesus then returns to the ancient metaphor of light,
enjoining his hearers not to hide their light under a bushel
(as we might perhaps say, in a closet), but to bring it out
so that it may shine clearly in front of all. He who, John
tells us, is "the light of men" does not want the light
wasted. This does not mean that we are to show off our
good deeds. A little later we are being specifically warned
against that. It does mean that we should go about cheer-
ing up others, not with mere smiling grimaces, but with
the shining forth of interior joy, the light within us that
is our spiritual being.

35 *Jesus Does Not Destroy the Karmic Law*

The teaching of Jesus, far from abrogating the moral
law expressed in the Torah and elsewhere in ancient liter-

ature, gets to the heart of it. When moral law is codified and set forth in a series of negative commandments ("Thou shalt not . . ."), and then interpreted like the Highway Code, its spiritual nature is easily forgotten. Law as administered in the courts out of a body of common law and statute or "black-letter" law may succeed in a rough, general way, in getting some sort of justice done. It is better than nothing, of course, and we are all thankful for it. But at the best it is a far cry from what even the least morally sensitive among us sees as full justice.

Jesus upholds the law in very definite terms. Not a comma, not an apostrophe, may be deleted from the Torah, so useful is it as an expression of the spiritual principle that is the moral law of the universe. On the contrary, Jesus insists on an interpretation that goes far beyond "the letter of the law."

For instance, we all know it is forbidden to murder; but Jesus does not talk of murders of the first or second degree, as do the law courts in our time. He looks inward. When you inwardly so hate as to wish a person dead, you have killed him and involved yourself in his murder (although no court will convict you) as surely as if you had inserted the knife or shot the pistol.

The Torah also explicitly forbids adultery and prescribes severe penalties for it. Jesus, however, says that lusting after a person *is* adultery. He goes through several other examples of laws that are, as we might say, "in the book," and shows that disobedience to them begins inside us. That is where the mischief lies. The administration of the law by the courts is by comparison only cosmetic. It attends to wrongs that issue in certain specific acts, for the courts do not and cannot pretend to see inside people's hearts. It does not get to the root of the evil, which is in the interior life.

36 *Swearing* MATTHEW 5.33-37

When we try to reinforce what we say by invoking the name of God or of a holy person or sacred shrine or book,

we are advertising that our plain word is not accounted
good enough. If our plain word is so unreliable, why
should anyone believe us if we support it with an oath?
Sometimes people prefix a statement with a phrase such
as "To tell you the truth," as though they were in the
habit of uttering falsehoods. Such asseverations cannot be
reassuring to any thoughtful person. How commendable,
then, is the Quaker practice of refusing to take an oath
even in court but, instead, simply to affirm.

What Jesus says here is an expression of a particular
attitude of mind that has always been commended by
holy men. A person who has genuine singleness of purpose and purity of heart can never need to support what
he says by uttering oaths.

37 Revenge and Love
MATTHEW 5.38-48   LUKE 6.27-36

Again, what Jesus counsels here is what the greatest
saints and sages have said, each in his own way. Revenge
is a natural instinct. It is the expression of an urge to see
justice prevail. If you give me a black eye, I retaliate by
giving you as good a shiner as you gave me. I can defend
my action in the name of justice and indeed the Torah
condones it in principle. Yet, "an eye for an eye" is not
the full expression of what lies behind the Torah, which
is summed up, as we have seen, in the law of love: love
God and your neighbor.

There is, however, a subtler reason for the path Jesus
commends, directing us to love our enemies, to turn the
other cheek, to render good for evil. Revenge in any
form is a waste of time. It is entirely negative. It accom-
plishes nothing useful. You demand my coat. Rather than
argue with you, wasting time and energy and fraying my
nerves, may it not be better in the long run to say, in
effect: "Go ahead—take my wardrobe if you must. Can't
you see I'm busy?"

Jesus gives an example in the case of one's being forced
to walk a mile. He should go two miles rather than refuse

or make a fuss. It may be that Jesus had in mind a soldier who might arouse a householder in the middle of the night asking for urgent transportation to the next village. Instead of grumbling, why not just do it as cheerfully as possible? Bring him back, too, if he wants it. The journey will seem shorter to both of you if you are pleasant about it. You will have lost less than if you made a great fuss over the matter. Behind these injunctions that Jesus gives is much prudential wisdom. Again, driving provides a modern illustration. If you insist adamantly on your rights you will charge ahead (as is your right), against the driver who is illegally trying to make a left turn in front of you, and then spend the rest of your life maimed and telling everyone you were in the right and what a bad driver he was. Yielding pays.

Yet beyond all such practical, prudential reasons in support of Jesus's teaching at this point, lies a more fundamental principle still. It is really the same principle that operates in "defensive" driving, but at a deeper level. The spiritual life is exacting, demanding infinite concentration and resolve. If you want to make progress in the interior life you must set aside all negative preoccupations, all that stands in the way of your supreme enterprise. In the monastic life certain rules are designed to assist in this commitment and resolve, for instance, silence. Most people waste an enormous amount of energy and time in fruitless talk, which disastrously interferes with commitment to any serious objective. This is not to say, of course, that we should become mute. Conversation is not only one of the finest pleasures of civilized life; it can be peculiarly creative. How little of our talk, however, is of that quality and how much of it worthless and sometimes even pernicious gossip!

I knew an American doctor who, just before he was going into his surgery to meet his patients, received a telegram informing him that his sister had been beheaded by the Japanese. As he opened the surgery door he saw his first patient, a Japanese-American. His natural instinct was to rage. Then suddenly (he was a deeply spiritual man) he saw the situation as a challenge and treated the patient with more than ordinary sympathy and care. I knew a lady whose son had been appointed to a position that another man had so coveted that the latter shot the son. Despite the intensity of her grief, she refused to assist in getting evidence to convict the suspect. What would all the toil and trouble and misery have accomplished? As she saw the situation, nothing. Her stance may have been right or wrong, but she perceived the nature of the principle we are considering here. Where the choice lies between destructive negativity and getting ahead with the main enterprise of life (the cultivation of our inner life and progress in spirituality), the negative choice should be unhesitatingly thrown out. So don't waste time on your enemy except by doing something constructive. Never waste time or energy on mere spite or vindictiveness. In all this, Jesus tells us, take God for your model. He does not discriminate. The sun shines on the unjust as on the just.

38   Doing Good Unnoticed

MATTHEW 6.1-8

Why not do good as publicly as possible? We have just been told to let our light shine before men. Is not doing good in secret much the same as hiding that light in the closet? No. We were enjoined to let light shine through us: the light that shines from within us whether we are doing anything or not. Showing off our good deeds is a very different matter.

We all like public admiration and perhaps even more the approval of our friends. By publicly heading the list of subscribers to a worthy cause we hope to win that approval, to make ourselves esteemed by those whose esteem we cherish. Every fund-raiser knows this motive well and capitalizes on it. Many churches formerly used discreet little velvet bags into which the widow could drop her mite without attracting the sidesman's attentive eye. The sad fact remains that the open plate brings better financial results. And if people like to show off their giving in public, they like even more to parade their fine deeds. What Jesus tells us is that, in the very act of showing off, the giving and the deeds become spiritually much depreciated in value, to say the least. For in the last resort, doing good is a very private affair not to be spilled out in public or exhibited like a Cadillac in a showroom. When good deeds are done in secret, seen only by the doer and God and the angels, the goodness motivating them drenches the souls as does rain the garden. Publicizing it erodes that moral goodness.

All this is even more acutely true of prayer. Jesus speaks of those who love to make a great show of their praying. They stand at street corners or elsewhere in the limelight, hoping to be noticed and approved. They are, he says, hypocrites, that is, play-actors. Conventional religion fosters such hypocrisy. "There is nothing more deadening to the divine," writes George MacDonald, "than a habitual dealing in the outsides of holy things." That is precisely what conventional religion inevitably fosters. The elimination of grandeur in ritual and ceremonial certainly does not in any way diminish the truth of that statement. Impoverished liturgy deals in the outsides of holy things no less effectively than any other kind.

That is not necessarily to say that public worship is to be avoided. On the contrary, it is a useful instrument in the development of the interior life. But unless it springs from the hearts of people who are already attuned to lonely prayer it can be nothing but a vain show. Jesus enjoins his hearers, when they pray, to go into their private room and lock the door, then pray in secret. He promises that God will "hear them in secret" but "reward them openly." The spiritual energy that is created through private prayer is so tremendous that its effects are bound to reverberate far and wide. Alas, many churchfolk do not know of the nature of such spiritual realities. If they did they would understand their value and see the futility of public prayer that is not grounded in a private walk with God.

39 *The Lord's Prayer*
MATTHEW 6.9-18   LUKE 11.1-4

The Lord's Prayer has been accepted in all Christian traditions as the model of true prayer. Many treatises have been written upon it. Here we may notice an underlying motif often overlooked. Failure to forgive others need not be considered a sin that God, when he sees it, punishes by withholding his forgiveness from us. It is rather that by not forgiving others we automatically exclude the forgiveness of ourselves. For the condition of forgiveness is a loving heart, which we, by our unforgiving attitude, have failed to attain.

This is a concept that is well known among exponents of the Ancient Wisdom. What Jesus expounds in this petition is an inexorable moral law. A loving heart that forgives others automatically melts the guilt in ourselves so that we are forgiven even as our heart goes out in love to others.

The petition for deliverance from evil or "the Evil One" (*apo tou ponērou*) reflects the deep awareness of the power of demonic agencies and of the importance of arming ourselves against them. They are part of the reality of the spiritual dimension. Through prayer we link ourselves to the creative power and therefore guard ourselves against the forces that are ever seeking our destruction. It is in the spiritual world that the fiercest battles take place.

40 *Fly Away, Care*
MATTHEW 6.19-34   LUKE 12.22-34

This beautiful passage expresses in several striking figures one of the most fundamental teachings of the Ancient Wisdom: detachment from the anxieties and cares of the world and from the stressful concerns that attachment to them creates.

We live in the physical world and are confronted daily and hourly by the exigencies of that circumstance. We need food, clothing, shelter, and many other things that go to make a full life. The wise man or woman is constantly aware of all that, but sees it all in perspective, taking care not to be ensnared by the world in such a way as to distort true spiritual values.

We all enjoy possessions, which can be useful instruments for our spiritual progress. Books and pictures, for instance, minister to our spiritual needs. The danger lies in excessive attachment to our possessions. Our only lasting treasure, Jesus reminds us, is in "heaven," in the spiritual dimension of being that is within us. We should invest in that, for such treasures are impervious to rust and termites. No burglars or robbers can steal them from us. They are our only safe investments and their yield is infinite. What we spend on "earthly" things should be accounted a temporary investment with a limited, temporary yield. Do not mistake the one kind of investment for the other. There is no way we can be absolutely committed to both God and money. Inside us is the eternal light, the divine light. Look out on the world through your senses, using them in such a way as to enhance that light and cause it to burn more and more brightly. For if you do not, you will be utterly dark inside, bereft of your most priceless treasure.

You ask for examples? Why not look at entities lower down than we on the evolutionary scale? They have less light inside, but they do not waste what they do have. Look at the birds in the sky! Are they worrying about their investments, their stocks, their bonds? Are they demanding pay raises? Do they lie awake at night wondering about their future? No, yet day by day they find their food. Or look at the flowers in the field! No dressmaker on earth could design anything more lovely, yet they never give it a thought. In their own way they trust in God. True, our situation is inevitably less simple; nevertheless, we must keep mindful of our real treasure and so fasten our eyes upon it that we do not allow ourselves to be seduced into mistaking the husk for the goodness inside. Only then shall we know on which side our true bread, the food of our souls, is buttered.

Unlike cats and dogs, we have entered into the dimen-

sion of time in such a way that we have to take account of
the past and the future. We cannot live for the fleeting
moment as does a bird on the wing. We cannot rely as do
birds and beasts on instinct, for we are endowed with reason. Yet this very endowment can become a source of en-
trapment, dragging us down into the soggy morass of the
world and causing our spirits to choke and die. What we
call life is worthless if we let its roots die within us while
we are tending the branches outside. Get at the roots and
the rest will take care of itself. As Nature cares for the
birds in the air and the flowers in the field, so God will
take care of us if only we keep our attention riveted on
the things that belong to our spiritual health. So tomorrow will look after itself if today we tend the light within
us. All this accords in every way with the wisdom handed
down to us by the sages of all religions. Here, as elsewhere in the "Sermon on the Mount" passages, Jesus
teaches very much the same wisdom as the others but in
his own inimitable way.

41   On Judging Others
MATTHEW 7.1-5   LUKE 6.37-42

Notoriously we find fault with other people easily,
while even the best of us discern faults within ourselves
only with the greatest difficulty. What is wrong with
others seems to stare me in the face; what is wrong with
me is veiled from me by my own disinclination to look. I
do not want to see anything wrong with me, since to find
it will mean a great deal of trouble to rectify what is amiss.
Self-criticism demands great spiritual maturity, because
we have a built-in instinct to veil ourselves from ourselves. Jesus uses a colorful comparison: the faults in
others are like two-by-fours and the faults in ourselves
like specks of sawdust. No doubt this imagery is right out
of the carpenter's shop. It is plainly jocose exaggeration of
the sort Jesus liked occasionally to use by way of emphasizing a point. The central point is that in judging other
people you are thereby setting the standard for yourself. A

loving and forgiving attitude to others will redound to yourself, while a harsh judgment will fill you with guilt about yourself that will lie festering in your unconscious mind. Once again the merciful bring mercy upon themselves. This is the karmic principle.

Luke introduces here a *mashal* or brief parable that Matthew brings in later in his Gospel (Matthew 23.16), but not in his version of the Sermon, about the blind leading the blind. If we hope to help other people in their spiritual progress, we must first be spiritually equipped ourselves. This is another way of saying that we should not go about looking for opportunities to criticize other people unless we are sure we are able to help them. This we certainly cannot do if we are in the same case as they.

42   *On Casting Pearls Before Swine*
MATTHEW 7.6

This verse has profound esoteric significance. The light we have with us, along with our whole spirituality, is an incomparable treasure. It is to be guarded from those who seek to destroy it out of ignorance or stupidity or envy. As there is no point in throwing pearls in front of pigs or handing edifying literature to dogs, so it is futile to talk about levels of spirituality to those who are unprepared. Not only are you wasting your time; you are doing no good to them. You would not give a two-year-old child a rare Bible to use. The child could not read it and would probably scrawl on it or tear it up. In later years he would reproach you for having been so irresponsible. You would wait, of course, till he is old enough to profit from such an item. So you should not in any cavalier way thrust great hidden truths on people not yet advanced enough to cope with them.

It is usually unwise and may be very wrong to interfere with the religious devotion of people who are attached to a form of religion that you may consider mere superstition. Gandhiji used to say of the idols used in popular religion in India that although he did not use them himself he would never stand in the way of their use by others who found them helpful. No, indeed! That would be like stopping a budding pianist from playing the five-finger exercises by giving him instead a score of Chopin. Much in all the religions of the world is baby-food. Paul fully recognized this. He told the Corinthians (I Cor. 3.2) that he had fed them with milk because they were babes, rather than with adult food that would have been beyond their capacity to chew. We are all at various stages of spiritual development, and the last thing we should do is to impose what is good for us on those who are not yet ready for it. To do so is tempting because we know how good it is for us. We must bear in mind that for us, too, at one time, what is now so good for us would not have been helpful at all.

43 *On Seeking Truth*

MATTHEW 7.7-11   LUKE 11.5-13

One of the greatest of spiritual insights lies in the recognition that truth is there waiting to be tapped as surely as water lies in the spring. Moreover, if we really want insight we have only to ask God for it and we shall receive it. Jesus, as elsewhere, speaks of God here as a Father. If a son asked his father for bread, would his father give him instead a snake? If parents know what to give their children, so our "heavenly Father" knows what to give us for our spiritual enlightenment and progress. So "ask and ye shall receive." We have only to turn inwards in heartfelt prayer and we shall find what we are looking for, what fits our needs and insures our progress. It is there for the taking, but we must seek it from within. How much treasure is there within us that we never use! It is lying there for us to take. Neurophysicists tell us there are vast areas of the human brain that are untapped: "virgin soil" ready to be tilled.

44 *The Golden Rule*

MATTHEW 7.12

This celebrated precept is found in the teaching of practically every great moral sage and religious teacher in the history of mankind. It is at the heart of the teaching of Confucius; nor was it original with him, for he inherited it from the ancient Chinese classics that long antedate the sixth century B.C. in which he lived. When Fan Ch'ih asked about humanity, Confucius said: "Love men." He went on to say that without humanity a person can neither endure adversity nor enjoy prosperity. *Jen*, this humane quality at the root of the Confucian ethic, is closely related to the quality of *shu*, which may be rendered "reciprocity." When Tzu Kung asked for one single principle for guidance in life, Confucius told him: "Do not do to others what you would not want others to do to you." (Analects, XV, 23) There are parallels in all the great religions of the world. The principle is well known to Western ethical thought in the teaching of Kant, whose "categorical imperative" expresses it in a somewhat more developed form. It is certainly not this injunction that gives the teaching of Jesus distinctiveness. That he used it in his teaching shows, however, along with much else, how fully he was in accord with the Ancient Wisdom.

The Golden Rule was already expressed in more than one form, however, in Jewish literature. "Do to no one what you would not want done to you," is explicitly stated in Tobit 4.15, one of the books in the Wisdom literature of the Bible. The great rabbinical leader Hillel, who flourished about 70 B.C. to about A.D.10, offers the maxim in almost exactly the same words, and there are other forms in Hebrew literature, so that Jesus did not have to go beyond his own tradition for the concept.

45 *The Narrow Way and the Wide One*
MATTHEW 7.13-14

There are two ways one may take in the pilgrimage of life, says Jesus: one narrow, one wide. The wide way leads to destruction and death, the narrow way to life. What are we to understand by this imagery? The wide road is plainly easier to take; it is presumably open and easily found. Many people take it. At first sight it seems the better way, while the other looks like a back road that is traveled by few. By taking the wide, obvious way, you go along with the crowd, which looks only at the outsides of things. The narrow way is certainly hard, but it is the only way if you are to make authentic spiritual progress.

Kierkegaard tells an amusing story that illustrates the difference between the two ways. He asks us to imagine a flock of geese who can talk and who arranged regular Sunday church services which they attended faithfully and at which one of the ganders preached. The theme of the sermon was the lofty destiny of the geese, the great goal set before them by their Creator. (Kierkegaard whimsically notes that every time this word was mentioned the geese curtsied and the ganders bowed their heads.) The preacher says that by the aid of wings they have been given, they can fly away to distant, beautiful lands, which are their proper habitat, for here they are but strangers and pilgrims. Every Sunday it was the same. As soon as the preacher had finished, each waddled home to attend to the affairs of the coming week. Every Monday they went about their business as usual, thriving, becoming plump and delicate, and on Martinmas Eve a number of them were duly killed and eaten. What kept the geese so smugly content with their way of life (the wide one) more than anything else were the stories that were whispered among them about a goose that had actually taken the preacher seriously. This one had experimented with the wings to which the preacher had so habitually alluded in the course of his homilies. It was a terrible death, they whispered. But they did not whisper on Sundays, because that would have interfered with the beauty of the sermon and would have made a farce of their worship. Among the geese, however, some seemed to be suffering and sad, losing weight, and not prospering like the others. On Mondays the other geese would whisper what they suspected: these silly geese were taking the preacher seriously and were in danger of the terrible fate that had befallen that goose that had such a fearsome end. And the whisperers in turn were duly eaten next Martinmas Eve, for they had become plump, delicate, and fat: just the kind of fowl that people like for a festive table. The geese who were not outwardly thriving were spared.

The story is typical of Kierkegaard's biting satire against the half-religious person who enjoys religion as though it were an electric blanket on a cold night. It shows us the nature of the wide road to which Jesus refers, which looks so safe and natural, not to say fashionable. The narrow way, the way to spiritual advancement, is always hard. Not without reason does it also often look insecure and dangerous, for it is in fact fraught with many perils. True, according to the Ancient Wisdom and also the Bible (though many neglect this aspect of biblical teaching), we are aided by invisible helpers, messengers of the divine Being. Evil powers also assail us, however, and the more progress we are making and the higher we are advanced, the more interest they have in our downfall. For they are at war with us and in battle it is usually better to capture a brigadier than to kill a corporal. The narrow way, then, is in every way a hard one. Our spiritual goals are not won without sacrifice, patience, and much toil. Jesus, as we shall see, promises his followers to protect and help them along the way; his followers, nevertheless, must walk it.

Mother Julian of Norwich, a fourteenth-century English mystic, claimed to have received a series of fifteen revelations in a period of five hours on May 8, 1373, followed by another vision the following day. She puts the matter thus: "He did not say you would not be tempested; he did not say you would not be travailed; he did not say you would not be afflicted. What he said was: 'You shall not be overcome.'" That is his promise for those who choose the way of life. It fits perfectly the fundamental teaching of the Ancient Wisdom.

46   *False Prophets*

MATTHEW 7.15-29, 8.1   LUKE 6.43-49

How does one tell a false prophet or teacher from an authentic one? The answer Jesus gives might be summed up in this way: you look at what he *is*. You would not expect to gather grapes from a scrawny bramble bush. What else would you expect of an evil man but that he should bring forth the evil that is all he has to offer? He will bring forth scrawny brambles as surely as will the bramble bush, while the grapevine will bring forth grapes. So how do you tell a true prophet from a false one? Look at what he produces. When a teacher or a school or a church brings forth nothing but hollowness and sorrow and dissension and pride, you know that you are dealing with what is spiritually bankrupt.

It is easy to talk religion. One can learn to say "Lord, Lord," as easily as a good actor can proclaim in a television commercial the merits of his sponsor's coffee or soap. Pay no attention to that foolish kind of chatter, however persuasive and slick the talk sounds. When, however, you find a teacher who is patently good within, listen most carefully, hanging on to every word, no matter how awkward his delivery or how bad his speech. What matters is not the vessel that carries the message but the freight that the vessel carries. Golden words may misdirect attention from the precious truths to the mere sweetness of the phrases. Paul tells the Corinthians (II Cor. 4.7) the reason he does not use fine phrases. It is so that attention may be focused on the truths he is proclaiming, not on the eloquence or rhetoric.

The proclamation of truth, however, is a two-way traffic. As only the authentic teacher can utter divine truths, so only the truly good can hear it. The good teacher holds a mirror to his hearers in which only the good can see God.

Jesus offers a parable. Those who live their religion have built their house on a rock that will withstand storms; those who do not, have built on sand and their houses will fall as soon as the storm comes. The houses may look alike, but only the man who has built on a rock knows the difference between the authentic and the inauthentic.

47   The End of the Sermon
MATTHEW 7.28, 8.1

Matthew tells us that when Jesus had stopped speaking the people were astonished at his style of preaching, because he spoke with authority, not as the scribes spoke. When he moved away, the crowds followed him. The people knew they were listening not to a scholarly disquisition or commentary, but to the very voice of God.

VI

MORE TEACHING AND HEALING

48 *Lord, I Am Not Worthy!*

MATTHEW 8.5-13 LUKE 7.1-10

When Jesus went into Capernaum a centurion came up to him and pled with him to cure his servant who was lying at home paralyzed and suffering much pain. Centurions in the Roman army were officers in charge of a hundred soldiers. Local military posts were usually under a centurion's command. This centurion is shown at once to have been a humane man, concerned for the well-being of a favorite servant of his. Jesus agrees to go to the house and cure the man. The centurion replies that he is not worthy to have so holy a man under his roof. Moreover, he feels it is not necessary, since he believes Jesus can cure him by simply saying the word there and then. So it is: the servant is cured at the instant Jesus speaks.

The centurion's reasoning is unusually interesting. He tells Jesus that he, being an army officer accustomed to giving orders and having them instantly obeyed, puts the situation of Jesus in analogy to that of his own. Jesus must have a legion of invisible helpers at his command.

The centurion is saying, in effect, that if *he* wished to carry out some military exercise or maneuver at a distance, he would not personally go there; he would delegate his authority and have his orders carried out. That is the army way. He is confident that Jesus can do the same in the spiritual domain. "Just give the word and my servant will be cured."

The reply much pleases Jesus, because it shows that the centurion understands, in his own way, how things work in the spiritual realm.

We have already seen that Jesus, in preparing for his public ministry, was attended by angels who came and ministered to him. Toward the end, in the Garden of Gethsemane, he is to rebuke one of his disciples for trying to intervene in his arrest by using force: "Do you think that I cannot appeal to my Father who would promptly send more than twelve legions of angels to my defense?" (Matthew 26.53) The Evangelists plainly assert an awareness of the realities of the spiritual world, constantly in the mind of Jesus but nowadays so often forgotten or misunderstood by those who profess to give him their allegiance. It is impossible even to begin to understand the life and work of Jesus without recognizing the ever-present reality of a realm around us, invisible to ordinary sight, in which spiritual agencies are very active indeed.

49 *A Widow's Only Son Resuscitated*
LUKE 7.11-17

When Jesus was entering the town of Nain (probably the modern village of Nein, near Nazareth), a young man was being carried out to be buried. When Jesus saw the mother's intense grief he told her not to cry. Then Jesus put his hand on the bier and, as the bearers stopped, he said: "Young man, I tell you to get up!" The man, believed to be dead, got up and began to speak. Everyone was awestruck and news of the wonder spread rapidly.

There can be little doubt that the doings of Jesus reminded his contemporaries of the accomplishments of Elijah and Elisha, the great prophets of old. The story

Luke tells embodies features of the raising of the son of
the widow of Zarephath by Elijah (I Kings 17.17-24) and
also of Elisha's raising of the son of the Shunnamite (II
Kings 4.17-22, 32-37).

Death, we know, is an event in the brain. Precisely
when it occurs is not so easily determined as people in
antiquity and indeed in recent ages supposed. A common
practice in quite recent times was to hold a mirror in front
of the person's mouth; if it showed no trace of breath, the
person was accounted dead. We may well suppose that
the young man's spirit was on the point of leaving his
body, but at the word of Jesus he was recalled.

50 *John the Baptist Asks About Jesus*

MATTHEW 11.2-19   LUKE 7.18-35

John, still in prison, sent a message to Jesus by way of
John's own disciples, asking: "Are you the One, or are we
to expect someone else?" Jesus tells John's disciples to go
back and let him know what is happening: the blind have
had their sight restored, the lame are walking, the lepers
are cured, and so forth. When John's disciples leave,
Jesus praises him. Plainly John was no ordinary man, certainly no popular preacher seeking applause. Rather, John
is a true prophet who rebukes the powerful, caring nothing for his own safety. He rebuked Antipas as Elijah
had rebuked Ahab. He goes on, in Matthew's account, to
say quite plainly: "and he, if you will believe me, is the
Elijah who was to return" according to the promise of the
prophet Malachi (Malachi 3.23). To this Jesus adds: "If
anyone has ears to hear, let him listen!" Surely the secret
is that Elijah has been reincarnated in the person of John
the Baptist.

Jesus laments that while ordinary people, including
tax-gatherers and the like, appreciated John, receiving
baptism from him, the Pharisees and the lawyers who
ought to have been spiritually alert, had declined it.
When John the Baptist went around wearing coarse
clothes and living abstemiously he was called crazy,
diabolically possessed. When Jesus goes around leading a

more moderate sort of life, eating and drinking and socializing, he is called a glutton, a drunkard who keeps company with sinners. Israel seems to be defeating the divine plan, repudiating first John, then Jesus. But Wisdom is vindicated by those who do listen and appreciate what tremendous spiritual events are occurring right under their noses. "Wisdom," it had been said (Proverbs 1.20), "calls aloud in the streets and lifts her voice in the squares; she calls out at the street corners . . . 'You ignorant people, how much longer will you cling to your ignorance?'" Jesus is allying himself not only to John, as his precursor or herald, but to the Ancient Wisdom literature with which he was so abundantly familiar and which pointed to the secret teaching he was now unfolding to those who had "ears to hear."

51 *A Harlot Learns the Mystery of Forgiveness*
LUKE 7.36-50

While Jesus was reclining at the table at a Pharisee's house, a woman of bad reputation entered and stood behind him. An intrusion of this sort was not so out of order as we might expect. In some Eastern countries people tend to wander into houses whenever the sound of music attracts them. In this case, however, the woman bursts out crying, letting her tears fall on Jesus's feet, then wiping them with her hair, kissing his feet over and over again and anointing them with perfume. The Pharisee, although he says nothing, is thinking to himself, "what kind of prophet is this Jesus if he cannot see what sort of woman he is allowing to caress him like this?"

The ability to read the thoughts of others is the mark of those far advanced in mastery of the spiritual life. Jesus has this capacity in a unique degree. Perceiving the Pharisee's unspoken reproach, he tells a story. There was a creditor who had two debtors, one owing him 500 denarii, the other fifty. He forgave both debts. Which would love him more? The one who owed more, of course. Then Jesus reminded the Pharisee that he, the host, had not bestowed any marks of affection on him. Yet this poor woman, certainly a great sinner, must have been forgiven her sins, because otherwise she could not have shown so much love. "Your sins *are* forgiven," he told the woman. Other guests at the table were offended at the notion that Jesus seemed to be claiming power to forgive sins. They missed the point.

In this beautiful story is revealed the mystery of forgiveness of sins through love. The story, like that of the Prodigal Son, is found only in Luke. Sinners such as this harlot have been forgiven much, and thus they are able to love much. Forgiveness comes to all who truly ask for it and the forgiveness creates repentance. We tend to think of the situation the other way around; but it is really the awareness of forgiveness that brings about the love. Only the forgiven know what it means to love God. That is why those who feel they have sinned much have a greater capacity to love God than many upright people who, having no adequate sense of forgiveness, can offer God only meager love. The woman in the story poured forth her love unrestrainedly and Jesus approved and encouraged her, saying: "Your faith has saved you; go in peace!"

52 *Women Follow Jesus*
LUKE 8.1-3

As Jesus and his twelve disciples go about the cities and villages, various women follow them. They seem to be all women who had been neurotic or psychotic and all had been cured by Jesus, including one particularly notable case, that of Mary of Magdala, a village on the southwest shore of the Lake of Galilee. She had "seven devils," signifying a very recalcitrant form of mental disorder, which Jesus had also cured. It often happens that people who have been through severe emotional turmoil or other mental distress develop unexpected spiritual perception. To live on an entirely even keel and, as we might say, "by the book," is often to blind oneself to the nature of the spiritual dimension of being. Only those who have been through tremendous upsets can make the leaps necessary to reach across that gulf that lies between the everyday kind of perception and glimpses of the greater dimension beyond.

53   *The Unforgivable Sin*

MATTHEW 12.22-45
MARK 3.19-30   LUKE 11.14-36

While Jesus was engaged in "casting out demons," the crowds were standing by, wondering and admiring. The Pharisees, however, charged that he cast out devils because he was acting under the power of Beelzebul, "the prince of the devils." Modern scholars, noting that the best Greek manuscripts read *beelseboul* (not *beelseboub* or *beelzebub* as rendered in traditional versions) identify the name with the fertility god of Ugarit, Aleyan Baal, called *zbl* in Ugaritic, meaning "prince." He is "the prince of this world," "the lord of the earth." The name was sometimes changed to "Beelzebub" ("Lord of the Flies") by the way of contempt. (See II Kings 1.2, where he is identified with "the god of Ekron.") In other words, Jesus is being charged with using worldy tricks rather than divine power.

This charge evokes from Jesus one of the severest rebukes he ever administered. To behold the destruction of evil such as mental illness and its replacement by wholeness, a cleansed state of being, and to disparage the transformation, attributing it to trickery, is to distort one's judgment so radically as to put one beyond the pale. It is to destroy the soul. Any other sin, any other wrongdoing, any false judgment, may be forgiven, but not this, because this is resistance to the known truth, the truth unfolded before your very eyes. A person so hardened as to take up this attitude would not be able to see the truth if it could be handed to him on a platter. He has already set his mind and heart against it through a resolve to adhere to his own prejudices. It is not a question of God's ability or willingness to forgive him; it is that he cannot permit himself ever to be forgiven, for he has, so to speak, torn out his own eyes. He cannot see the spiritual verities and nothing could ever make him see them. He is doomed to destruction.

In another story that Luke tells (Luke 16.19-31), a rich man in hell begs Abraham to send someone to his brothers to warn them, so that they may not have the same fate that he is suffering. Abraham tells the man that his brothers have Moses and the prophets to guide them. The man protests that they will not listen, but if somebody rose from the dead and told them, then they would listen. No, Abraham insists: if they won't listen to Moses and the prophets, they won't listen even if someone came back from the grave to warn them.

In these teachings Jesus discloses one of the most profound spiritual truths in the Gospels. If you allow your mind to close itself definitely against the truth, your case is hopeless. You can never again hear the heavenly music, because you will be deaf to it. You may make mistakes, terrible mistakes, as we all do; but if only you keep an open mind to spiritual reality you will in time win through to progress in the spiritual life. Otherwise you will fall by the wayside as surely as did the dodo and the dinosaur in the biological aspect of evolution.

A woman in the crowd, hearing Jesus speak, threw him a compliment saying that happy was the mother who had borne and suckled him. But Jesus took the opportunity of making the riposte: ''Still happier are those who hear the word of God and keep it!'' He was indirectly rebuking the Pharisees. When people demand a sign, he told the crowd, they will get none. For people with open minds will be given signs in plenty and those with closed minds will explain away any sign that could ever be given them.

Luke repeats here the parable of the lamp that he tells elsewhere (8.16-18; see below at Section 54) and that Matthew puts within his version of the Sermon on the Mount. It illustrates the theme that all the Synoptics treat: the unforgivable sin. ''See to it then,'' says Jesus, ''that the light inside you is not darkness.''

54 *Spiritual Kinship*
MATTHEW 12.46-50   MARK 3.31-35   LUKE 8.19-21

All the Synoptists recount a story of Jesus being told, while he was speaking to the crowds, that his relatives were waiting outside and wished to speak with him. Characteristically, he replied to the effect that his real kin were his disciples. It is often said that "blood is thicker than water," and most people are well aware of the strength of family ties. Love of parents for their children, of children for their parents, of all of those close to them in family relationship, is an admirable disposition. Most of us would despise anyone notably lacking in it. Yet spiritually perceptive and mature people know that there is a kinship far more binding than even the closest family tie, a spiritual kinship, which produces overwhelming love of a far purer and deeper kind.

This arises from a circumstance well known to all who understand that each one of us, though born into a family and so inheriting the genes of the family ancestry, has a soul that "cometh from afar." This spiritual affinity that the soul has for other souls far transcends in every way even the finest of family bonds. Many of us, indeed, feel strangers even among the family that we love and cherish while feeling instantly at home with others genealogically remote from us. Friendship can be an even holier relationship than "flesh-and-blood" ties, especially when it relates to a long reincarnational history.

In the reincarnationist view which is so much a part of the Ancient Wisdom, we choose our own parents, and therefore we are in some way attached to them both spiritually and biologically. But while we may have little in common with others (brothers and sisters, for instance) who share the same ancestry, we may find profound kinship with persons coming from an entirely foreign background. What is related here of the attitude of Jesus is an enunciation of a great truth arising from the nature of our karmic history and of our spiritual destiny.

55 *A Collection of Parables*
MATTHEW 13.1-52 MARK 4.1-34 LUKE 8.4-18

All the Synoptists put together several parables of Jesus and include with them a question the disciples asked about parable-telling, to which Jesus gives a peculiarly significant reply. The question in the minds of the disciples may be expressed thus: Why do you teach spiritual verities by this oblique method instead of doing so plainly and directly? Mark says specifically that the question was put when Jesus was alone with a few disciples after the crowd had gone. The answer reported in all three Synoptics is the same: to you the mysteries of the spiritual realm are revealed directly; to others it has to be done by way of parables or allegories. To many people the story will remain enigmatic. They will treat it as a sort of riddle, because their minds are closed. Trying to express the truth to them is like trying to tell a Walt Disney cartoon about the third dimension. The task is hopeless. Jesus quotes Isaiah (Isaiah 6.9), where that prophet was told to dull the minds of the people that "they may see but not perceive, listen but not understand." We need not interpret this as meaning that God closes the minds of the masses so that they will not be able to perceive spiritual truths. On the contrary, people do it themselves, so that when divine truths are revealed they cannot possibly understand, no matter how the revelation is unfolded to them. Through parables, however, some will be led to see the point and grasp the nature of the spiritual world.

The word mystery (*mystērion*) that is used in all three Synoptics in this connection, though occurring often in Paul's letters, appears in the Gospels only here. It means a truth that is not immediately apparent to people accustomed to confining their apprehension of reality to the empirical world but is disclosed to those who have the capacity to go beyond that mode of apprehension. The whole passage proclaims in a most striking way that spiritual teaching is by its very nature the teaching of hidden, esoteric knowledge such as is dealt with in theosophical traditions. A mystery is neither completely concealed nor completely revealed; that is to say, it is not inscrutable nor is it disclosed with the clarity of a mathematical proposition such as two plus two equals four. It has to be probed and for this we have to develop a new mode of apprehension, a new sort of intellectual tongs. We cannot catch a rainbow with the kind of tongs used for picking an object out of a store window. Our whole approach must be radically different. If it be so with the rainbow's light, how much more so with the truths of the spiritual realm? People's capacity for grasping such truths varies enormously, depending on their degree of maturity and advancement. Many are so deaf to the music of the spirit that even if all nine choirs of angels were to sing it into their very ears within the range of an inch they would either take no notice or, at most, turn around to see whether someone had left on the television on low volume. Others will start at the flutter of an angel's wing.

The parables among which this trenchant passage on the nature of revelation is set are well known. The first is the parable of the sower, some of whose seeds fell on the wayside and were eaten by the birds, while others fell on to rocks where there was not enough earth to sustain them, and others again among the thorns, with which they could not compete, being eventually choked. Some seeds, however, fell on good soil and grew up to yield good fruit, some a hundredfold, some sixtyfold, some thirtyfold.

All the Synoptists, after recounting this parable, add, "Listen, anyone who has ears to hear." The ears called for are, of course, not the ears that stick out of our heads providing the intricate instrument through which we apprehend sound, but an inward instrument of even greater delicacy and sensitivity. Further, all four narrators provide a sort of interpretation of this parable which, however, would be incomprehensible to those who do not know the meaning of the "Kingdom" to which the interpretation refers as its root metaphor. If one's olfactory sense is weak, a descriptive analysis in words with auditory or visual analogies might help in its development; but if the sense is irreparably withered, nothing can bring it to life. So even the interpretation of a parable is of use only to those capable of profiting from it. Herein lies the hidden meaning of the notion of "election" in predestinationist theology: only a minority can understand a spiritual disclosure at any level. Most are not ready for it, being able to receive only milk, not solid food, as in the case we considered earlier, or else they have self-destructed.

Luke introduces here the parable about putting a lamp under a bed rather than bringing it out in the open, also used by him elsewhere (11.33-36). He follows the same line as Mark in affirming that we must take care *how* we hear: anybody who has spirituality will get more, and from those who, lacking it, think they have it, even what they think they have will be taken away. In other words, spiritual insight, no less than physical stength, grows with exercise. If you don't exercise your spirituality, it will atrophy as surely as a muscle you don't use. Nor will you notice the gradual departure of its power while it is taking place. Many years ago a horse kicked me in the shin, resulting in a fractured tibia, and I was in a cast for many weeks. When I was released from the cast I jumped to the floor, only to find that I had temporarily lost much of the power in that leg, which took weeks to recover by exercise. A scholar related to me that when he received a university appointment he put his religious faith in a drawer of his mind so as to maintain the objectivity he wanted in his academic discipline; ten years later when he went back to the "drawer" it was empty. Spirituality is not like a gold nugget that you can put in a safe deposit at the bank and withdraw fifty years later. Like all living realities, it must grow or wither.

In Matthew, Jesus uses further variations to bring out the meaning of "the kingdom of heaven." It is like a mustard seed, tinier than any other seed known to the farmer; yet it grows into something so large that the birds nest in it. It is also like a hidden treasure that a man finds, causing him to sell everything he has to acquire title to the field in which the treasure lies. It is like a pearl so precious that a pearl merchant sells his whole stock to acquire it. It is also like a net that gathers up all sorts of things from the sea, which then have to be sorted out, the good on one side, the worthless on the other. So the angels will come and separate those who have attained spirituality from those who have failed to do so. They will keep the former and throw the rest into the trash can.

Then Jesus asks the disciples if they have really understood and they say they have. Finally he tells them that every scribe who becomes a disciple of spirituality is like a householder who brings from his storeroom "things both new and old."

Here Matthew provides us with a striking image of the resources in a treasure-store of wisdom, some of which are or seem new, while others were known to the sages of antiquity. The professional scribal schools in the ancient world were the centers where the wisdom literature was developed and transmitted. The scribes were a motley crew in the sense that some were mere hacks and probably snobbish ones at that, arrogantly proud of their elevation above the social level of manual workers, while others were deeply spiritual men who really imbibed the wisdom they had in their custody and transmitted it. So there were good and bad among them as there are good and bad librarians and good and bad museum curators in our own time, and as there were good and bad sophists in the days of Socrates. Jesus, whom the scribes approved when he inveighed against the Sadducees, rebuked the scribes for their professional limitations, for being unworthy to deal in the wisdom that was their stock-in-trade, as Socrates had despised the sophists who were unworthy of their profession, a profession he so splendidly represented. Though Jesus disdained the scribes who abused their office as custodians of the wisdom they traded in, he certainly did not disdain the wisdom in which they traded.

56 Stilling the Storm
MATTHEW 8.18, 23-27   MARK 4.35-41   LUKE 8.22-25

Once again Jesus is in a boat. Some have even suggested that his movements on land may have been subject to some restriction, but there is no hard evidence for this. At any rate, all three Synoptists relate that Jesus, after getting into the boat with his disciples, falls asleep. Then a storm arises (squalls from the neighboring hills are com-

84

mon in the region) and the disciples arouse their Master.
Does he not care that they are all going to be drowned?
Jesus, having awakened (Mark says he slept on a cushion
at the stern), greets the wind and the sea with a *shalom*,
the salutation of peace one gives to a friend. "Peace, be
still," he says. The storm abates. The awed disciples ask
what kind of man is this who can subdue the elements of
nature. As the King James Version renders their question
in its picturesquely antique cadences, "What manner of
man is this, that even the winds and the sea obey him?"
The Hebrew people had no word for nature, attributing its
manifestations directly to God who "plants his footsteps
in the sea and rides upon the storm." So who could subdue a storm, making the wind and sea obedient to his
will but one in whom is invested the divine power itself?

57 *The Maniacs and the Pigs*
MATTHEW 8.28-34 MARK 5.1-20 LUKE 8.26-39

The location of the incident is uncertain because of textual variancies in the manuscripts, but for our purpose
this is unimportant. The accounts do not agree,
moreover, whether Jesus encountered one maniac or two;
Matthew says two, Mark and Luke say one.

All agree, however, on the substantial facts about the
maniacal condition and how Jesus dealt with it. The
maniac is of an extremely violent type who, having fled
from human society, haunts the rock-hewn graves on the
hillside and, in a sort of suicidal frenzy, cuts himself with
stones. Jesus asks the man his name and the man replies
enigmatically, "Legion," presumably meaning that all
sorts of entities are in him; he is what modern
psychiatrists would call a multiple personality type. He
then begs Jesus not to send away the demons that are in
him but, if he must, then let them go into the herd of pigs
that are within sight.

The notion that evil spirits could be transferred from
one embodiment to another was a very common belief
that even found expression in an old Aramaic exorcistic

formula: "Off with you and fall upon the gazelles on the hills!" Jesus responds accordingly, exorcizing the evil spirits and letting them enter the pigs who rush headlong into the water, killing themselves, while the maniac now sits at the feet of Jesus fully restored in mind.

Jesus here as elsewhere fully recognizes the power of both evil and good agencies. Evil agencies seek to take possession of a body and torment or even destroy its rightful inhabitant. In the case in point many such evil agencies had taken possession, causing extremely severe mental disturbance and a tendency to violence. The phenomena, so familiar in modern psychiatry and parapsychology, are certainly well described in terms of the ancient mode of delineating the situation. The maniac has "lost his mind." It has been supplanted by wild energies that are out of control. Typically, he leaves the haunts of men and wanders in ghoulish fashion among the graves of the dead, tearing his clothes and trying to rip himself open with sharp stones, potentially at once homicidal and suicidal.

The inhabitants, terrified at the exorcistic powers of Jesus, beg him to leave the region. How characteristic of the spiritually immature, who so often do not know their friends from their foes! Finally we are told that the man wants to follow Jesus, but Jesus declines, urging him to go home and tell his family and friends of the wonderful cure he has experienced.

58 Who Touched Me?
MATTHEW 9.1,18-26 MARK 5.21-43 LUKE 8.40-56

Jesus now returns to his own city where he meets Jairus, one of the rulers of the synagogue. Jairus is in great distress: his daughter, he says, is dying—probably dead by now. If only Jesus will come and touch her she will live. As Jesus goes to the house, crowds of people follow to see what he will do.

A most remarkable incident is recounted as occurring on the way to the house of Jairus. A woman in the crowd, convinced that if only she can get near enough to Jesus to touch his clothes, the power in him will cure her of a hemorrhage from which she has suffered for twelve years. Suddenly Jesus, "aware that power had gone out from him," turns and looks around him, asking his disciples, "Who touched me?" The disciples, knowing that the crowds were pressing in on Jesus from every side, thought the question strange. Why, he was surrounded by people, *all* touching him! In the Middle East people are temperamentally disposed to touching other people, even strangers with whom they wish to be friendly or whom they find at least interesting. But Jesus knew that someone had not merely touched him but had actually withdrawn power from him, calling upon the supply of divine energy within him. Here is a very vivid expression of the attitude of Jesus to his healing work and to the whole question of the nature of the spiritual dimension. That people should be touching him was of no account in itself. They did it all the time as they surrounded him wherever he went, as occurs with almost anyone who attracts attention. But he was aware that someone had touched him with the express intent of drawing upon the divine energy within him. At last, in response to his continued inquiries, the woman owns up, falling at his feet and telling him the whole story and of her instant cure. Jesus blesses her, telling her that it was her trust that cured her. Now she should go in peace, forever free of her former affliction.

This is certainly a most extraordinary story, since the cure is effected without Jesus's saying any words or performing any gesture. The woman draws upon him as one would draw water from a well or pour oil from a bottle. Most astonishing still, Jesus, according to the narratives, does not seem to know who did it, yet he knows that the divine energy (*dynamis*) in him had been tapped and withdrawn. This energy, we are to understand, is proceeding from him in such a way that it pours forth from his body. Even his clothes retain some of it. This is of course a notion very familiar in parapsychological inquiry and known throughout the ages in theosophical circles. No doubt the woman has heard of it. But that the Evangelists should represent Jesus at the center of the scene of a great parapsychological drama, the focus of a spiritual reality that lies all around us, is of the greatest interest. It is of that spiritual reality that his true disciples acclaim him Lord.

Continuing on to the house of Jairus, Jesus hears people telling Jairus that since his daughter was now dead there was no point in troubling the Master any more. Jesus reassures them saying, "Don't be afraid, just have faith." As he goes in and finds people shrieking inconsolably, he asks, "Why all the commotion? The child is only sleeping." They laugh at this and he turns them all out of the house except the child's father and mother and the few disciples Jesus has brought into the house with him. Then, going to the bedside of the child, he takes her by the hand and says, "Talitha, kum!" (Mark gives the words in Aramaic, as Jesus would have said them: "Little girl, get up!") The twelve-year old child gets up and begins to walk about. He asks the amazed parents not to tell anybody about it and to get her something to eat.

59 *More Cures* MATTHEW 9.27-34

As Jesus was walking, two blind men come after him, crying out to be cured of their blindness. They follow him into the house, where Jesus asks them whether they really believe. As always, the belief of the patient is essential. So also, however, is the healer's ability to perceive whether the belief they profess is genuine. Jesus restores their sight and charges them not to tell anybody, an injunction that they promptly disobey.

Then a man possessed of an evil spirit that is inhibiting his speech is brought to him. Jesus exorcizes the evil spirit and the man's speech is restored. Once again the Pharisees allege that he casts out devils by the power of the prince of devils, that is, by trickery.

60 *Again Rejected in his Home Town*
MATTHEW 13.54-58   MARK 6.1-6

When Jesus returns to his home town and teaches in the synagogue, people are still murmuring that this is the

carpenter's son. How can he have come by "this wisdom?" And once again he quotes the proverb that a prophet is honored everywhere except in his home town.
Although he cures a few sick people, he is not able to do
any great wonders. The incredulity of the people gets in
the way, for as all healers know, only in an atmosphere of
trust is spiritual healing possible. All healing depends in
great measure on the trust of the recipient. The healer is
simply an agent of the divine energy.

The local people cannot bring themselves to see Jesus
as he is perceived by others not affected by prejudices.
They keep coming back to the old story: he is the carpenter's son. How readily unspiritual people judge everyone and everything by origins rather than by actual
accomplishments. How can Jesus, a village lad, be a
prophet? The image of him as they have seen him in the
carpenter's shop interferes with their perception of what
he is doing, of what he really is. Again and again people
judge by externals, unable to penetrate to the inner
spirituality.

61 *Directions to the Disciples*
MATTHEW 9.35-11.1   MARK 6.6-13   LUKE 9.1-6

Jesus now resumes his travels, going about the cities
and villages, teaching and healing. He finds, however,
that the crowds are growing so large that he must make
his disciples instruments of the divine power. Assembling
them, he gives them instructions. They are not to go to
the Gentiles or to the Samaritans but, rather, to the "lost
sheep" among their own people, who will receive them.

For equipment they are to carry only the essentials, the
clothes they wear: no wallet or purse or spare clothing.
Their style of life must symbolize the faith by which they
are to live. Once again, detachment from the world is the
key. Worldly possessions can be burdensome. Jesus warns
them that they are going out as lambs among wolves.
They must beware of people, learning to be as wise as
serpents yet as harmless as doves. The principles are the
same as those collected and set forth in the Sermon on

Mount. They must expect to be persecuted, but in the end they will reap the supreme reward, their salvation, for they are already on the path to advancement in the spiritual realm. If they are persecuted in one city, they are to leave and flee to the next. Jesus reminds them that God knows even the number of hairs on their heads and that not even a little sparrow falls without God's knowledge, so they are constantly guided by benevolent agencies in the spiritual realm who are there to guard and protect them in their apostolate.

Nor are they to be surprised if their healing and teaching should stir up strife, for he has not come to make everything rosy, but to bring the sword of the spirit. Preachers who bring nothing but soothing messages know nothing of the nature of the spiritual realm, which cannot but bring about strife among those who seek to be advanced in it, for evil agencies are aroused as soon as good is performed or truth taught. This is indeed the Ancient Wisdom out of which was to spring the medieval proverb: "Where God builds his Church, the devil also builds his chapel." Of course! It is his most convenient place of doing business. Jesus is training his disciples to be not only his ambassadors but independent agents of the divine power.

62 John the Baptist is Executed
MATTHEW 14.1-12   MARK 6.14-29   LUKE 9.7-9

News of the doings of Jesus reached Herod the tetrarch. His wife Herodias, formerly his brother's wife, had been offended at John's denunciations of their marriage and indeed was still trying to have him killed. Herod, however, was afraid of John's spiritual power, for some said he was a reincarnation of Elijah. He wondered, too, if John's power might have been transferred to Jesus, about whom there was so much talk.

One evening there was a great banquet at which the daughter of Herodias danced in such a way as to capture all the guests, pleasing them so much that Herod offered the girl anything she cared to ask as a reward for her performance. The girl, prompted by her mother, asked for the head of John the Baptist on a plate. Herod, though grieved at his own rash promise, acquiesced and the girl was able to deliver to her mother the head of John on a plate.

The gruesome story symbolizes the indifference and cruelty of the world toward its greatest prophets. Because of cruel spite at a rebuke, a woman had contrived to force a prophet's execution. No wonder Jesus warned his disciples against the ways of the world, of people who, for a dance or a song, would destroy them merely because they do not like to hear the truth about themselves. When spiteful passions are aroused, justice and reason are the last things to come forth. That is why the passions of men and women can work such havoc at the very moment that great and good deeds are being performed. The seven deadly or "capital" sins recognized by our medieval forebears seem fairly innocuous when we talk about them dispassionately. Pride, envy, avarice, gluttony, anger, lust, and sloth sound mere blemishes in a character. Yet they can and often do lead not only to great human tragedies but to monstrous injustice and wicked treachery. They are the enemies of the spiritual life, for their presence causes men and women to enlist a host of evil agencies against the noblest of heroes and the dearest of saints only to mollify the anger in themselves or gratify their envious rage or insane ambition. Such people are the Devil's dupes and the adversaries of wisdom. Those who have learned from her are well aware of the danger they pose and they seek to rout out such dispositions from their hearts. The fate of John the Baptist stands as a grisly reminder of their evil power.

63 *Feeding Crowds with a few Loaves and Fish*
MATTHEW 14.13-23, 15.32-38   MARK 6.3-46, 8.1-9
LUKE 9.10-17   JOHN 6.1-51

Jesus, finding that crowds were following him, talked to them, teaching them at length. It was getting late in the day and they were in a desert place. The disciples therefore suggested to Jesus that he should send the people away to get something to eat in the nearest village. Jesus replied, "Feed them yourselves!" The disciples, having only five loaves and a couple of fish, protested that it was impossible to feed so many people with so little food. Jesus, however, told the disciples to have the people sit down in groups of about fifty each (according to Luke's version). Then, taking the five loaves and two fish, he blessed and broke the food in ritual fashion, giving thanks for it. He then handed it to the disciples to pass around the crowds. After the crowds had eaten, twelve baskets of food remaining were gathered up.

This story is recounted by all four Evangelists and, although most Bible readers have always assumed that the loaves and fish are supposed to have been miraculously multiplied, not one of the Evangelists actually asserts anything of the sort.

Surely what happened can be explained otherwise. Country people all over the world, and certainly not least the peasantry of countries in the Middle East, are of a suspicious turn of mind. They have little confidence in strangers. When they go out for any sort of lengthy excursion they take food with them, but they are too shrewd to display their provisions to the world at large. They hide these in their clothes, then take off in huddles with their close friends, fearing that if others see that they have food, they will be pestered to share it, leaving almost nothing for themselves.

Bearing this in mind, we may go on to suggest, very plausibly I think, that Jesus persuaded them all to bring out their own food and eat it openly, assured that there would be plenty for everybody and nobody would go away hungry. So indeed there was, since twelve baskets of food were gathered up after all had eaten. If one should say, "Oh is that all? No miracle?" we must answer, as in the case of the other story about the changing of water into wine, "If you think it's easy, just *you* try it with a crowd of oriental peasants!" Persuading people to trust one another is never an easy matter. From all that we know of the Person and work of Jesus, he would achieve it by the use of the energy streaming through him from the love at the core of all things. As in his healing Jesus transcended the art of medicine as commonly practiced, so in his feeding of the multitudes he transcended crowd psychology as commonly understood.

The story of the feeding of crowds with a few loaves and fish is repeated in a slightly different form and in a different setting in both Mark and Matthew. Each of these relates to a time by which Jesus had withdrawn for awhile to a place farther north, as far as possible from the public so as to be with his disciples alone. The second account does not fit the setting in which it is placed. Much scholarly discussion has been devoted to this and similar difficulties by way of trying to unravel the editorial processes that have brought about such confusion. Once again we must bear in mind that we do not have a clear historical narrative of the life and work of Jesus but, on the contrary, a potpourri of illustrative material out of which we have to try to find some sort of chronological order. Above all, however, we must recognize here and elsewhere the point much emphasized throughout this study: the Evangelists, even apart from the editorial processes that have occurred, could never have purported to provide us with a precise historical account but, rather, with a dramatic picture based upon the remembrance of his doings.

64 *Walk on the Water*
MATTHEW 14.24-36   MARK 6.47-56   JOHN 6.16-21

Of all the miracle stories in the Gospels, none has so captivated the popular imagination as has the story of Jesus's walking on water. For many it has become paradigmatic of all the miracle stories of the Bible. For many believers it represents the victory of Jesus over gravity and space; for skeptics it is the ultimate absurdity. There are indeed serious discrepancies in the accounts. Luke, moreover, omits the story entirely.

The critical mind is naturally disposed to suspect the invention of a legend; yet the motive for inventing so strange-sounding a story is difficult to imagine, presenting as many puzzles as the story itself. The Gospels were written primarily to persuade and attract pagans to the Christian Way. Why invent a story that seems to have no theological significance as do the birth and resurrection narratives, but seems calculated only to induce incredulity in the minds of ordinary readers accustomed to thinking in naturalistic terms? Moreover, unlike the healing miracles and the feeding of the multitudes, this story seems pointless. We have seen over and over again that miracles in the Bible are characteristically signs, showing forth the goodness and love of God, not mere marvels for the sake of the marvellous. New Testament scholars, try as they will, do not seem to provide any satisfactory explanation of what the miracle is intended to show, what religious value it might have, whether historically factual or not.

Only a parapsychological explanation appears to meet the case. Consider what is recounted and some of the discrepancies. Matthew and Mark both have Jesus eventually enter the boat from the sea on which he has been walking a considerable distance. Matthew even has Peter walking out of the the boat to meet Jesus, losing his nerve as he feels a heavy gust of wind, and crying out that he is sinking, whereupon Jesus stretches out his hand and saves him. John, however, makes no mention of Jesus's actually entering the boat at all.

So far as we can harmonize the accounts, it would seem that we are to suppose that Jesus stayed behind on land because he wished to pray, letting the disciples go on by themselves. By all acounts it was evening when they started out and dark by the time they saw Jesus on the water. By all accounts, too, the wind was strong and the sea rough. According to John, the disciples wanted to take Jesus aboard, but they reached the shore too soon, suggesting that they were there, as we might say, "before they could look around." Both Mark and Matthew report that the disciples cried out in fear, saying "It's a ghost!" (phantasma). Jesus does not contradict this. What he does, according to the Evangelists, is to encourage them to lay aside their fears: "It is I! Don't be afraid."

Might not this point to the only plausible interpretation? We have seen over and over again that Jesus shows every sign of unique psychic powers, which he always uses for a good purpose, never whimsically or, as we might say, "for fun." The discrepancies in the accounts might well arise from conflicting recollections of what was seen through the darkness in the midst of a fierce storm in which the boat was being heavily tossed in the sea. What they saw could well have been the projection by Jesus of the subtle body, a feat well known among all accustomed to psychic phenomena. In this interpretation, what the disciples saw would indeed have been a reality (a very vivid one) but, being still novices in the spiritual realm and at the same time under severe pressure from the forces surrounding them in the physical world and upsetting their equilibrium, they would be too bewildered to appreciate what was happening. This interpretation would be much less remarkable, from a parapsychological standpoint, than many of the other wonders related in the Gospels, some of which we have already considered.

When Jesus and his disciples arrived in Gennesaret, the local people recognized Jesus and began bringing the sick to him so that they might touch the edge of his cloak. Those who did so were completely cured. The same spiritual power was at work, we recall, in the case of the woman with the hemorrhage. Even his clothes are charged with the energy that is constantly exuding from him.

65 *Two Kinds of Bread*

JOHN 6.22-71

Jesus tells his hearers that there are two kinds of bread. There is the kind made out of barley or wheat that we eat for the nourishment of our bodies. We work for that bread. But there is another kind of work and another kind of bread to be worked for. He reminds them that their fathers had received manna in the desert. It was not Moses who provided that bread but God. That bread is "the true bread, the bread of God" that "gives life to the world." His hearers say, "Give us some of that bread!" and Jesus replies, "I am the bread of life." He goes on to speak of this bread much as he spoke to the Samaritan woman of "the living water."

Jesus, trying to wean his hearers from their habit of thinking of what was done in the past, emphasizes the present, indeed the ever-present character of the gift of this heavenly bread. "I have come down from heaven," he says. "I *am* the bread of life." This is a way of expressing the notion that the divine energy in him is the bread he is talking about. His hearers have the same difficulty with the notion of his "coming down from heaven" that Nicodemus had with "a birth from above." The stumbling block is accentuated by the fact that they know him as "the son of Joseph." They know his parents. How can he dare say he had "come down from heaven?" Jesus, hearing them murmuring and chattering among themselves on those lines, sees that there is no way of getting across spiritual ideas to people so geared to empirical ones that they insist on interpreting everything according to their own narrow minds.

"I tell you most solemnly," he goes on, "everybody who believes has eternal life." This bread he is talking about is living bread, and anyone who eats it will have eternal life. It is the spirit that gives life. He now speaks sacramentally: he knows he has come into this world as "the Word made flesh" (John 1.14) and he recognizes that the "flesh" is sanctified by the spirit, which is a basic idea in all sacramental theology. The divine energy in him that gives life radiates through his body and, we have seen, even through his clothes. To partake of his flesh is to partake of his spirit, for spirit, like light, cannot be enclosed in a box apart from all else.

This is a new concept for his hearers. They find it utterly absurd, so much so that some who had been following him give up and leave him. According to John,

96

Jesus already knew that one of the twelve would betray him and which one it would be: the one whom he knew was not grasping his message. At the Last Supper, at which he is to give the bread and wine to his disciples sacramentally, he is to declare explicitly that one will betray him and is to make clear that it is to be Judas. The present passage is traditionally taken to be a foreshadowing of that sacramental meal that was to become the central focus of all Christian worship.

Jesus, seeing that he has lost some of his followers, asks the twelve: "How about you? Are you also going to leave?" To this Peter gives the reply that is a classic utterance for Christians, "Lord, whom shall we go to? You have the message of eternal life." Jesus reminds them that he has chosen them, yet one of them is evil. He seems to be giving Judas an opportunity to withdraw, an opportunity that Judas ignores.

66   Hygiene, Spiritual and Physical
MATTHEW 15.1-20   MARK 7.1-23

Pharisees and scribes from Jerusalem note that some of the disciples of Jesus ate without the ceremonial washing of hands that Jewish tradition demanded. Jesus, as we have seen in other connections, held the Law in high respect; nevertheless, the principle of the Sabbath being made for man, not man for the Sabbath, always prevailed in his outlook. So the custom of washing before eating, which is obviously a desirable practice by any standards if only for physical hygiene, was in itself a good one. Jesus perceived, however, that his critics were merely trying to find a pretext for calling him a lawbreaker, and he retorted by calling them hypocrites, since, as he pointed out, some of the traditions they upheld were really ways around the divine commandments themselves. This, by the way, is the only place where Mark puts the word "hypocrite" into the mouth of Jesus. He is accusing them of playing at their religion by making a fuss over a trivial ceremonial neglect while habitually making havoc with the spirit of the divine law.

Jesus expresses his disparagement of their attitude by saying that it is not what goes into a person from the outside that defiles that person; it is what comes out. By this he meant that certain foods prohibited by the Jewish dietary laws and various other ways of keeping oneself ceremonially and ritually "clean" are worthless unless they are used as symbols of the real cleansing that must take place in the soul. It is when a man's thoughts are impure and his motives corrupt that he gives forth evil as surely as a dirty kettle gives off rust, no matter how clean the water you put in it. In short, the trouble begins inside, not outside. Can't you see, he says, that what goes into a person's mouth passes into his stomach and thence is excreted and goes into the sewer? It does not affect his spirit. It cannot defile his soul. From within, however, proceeds all the foulness that corrupts not only the soul of man but everything he touches and does. It is from inside, not outside, that come all the vile intentions that issue in murder, theft, adultery, envy, and every other kind of malice and misconduct.

All this is very much in the spirit of Jesus's general attitude toward external observances. In themselves there is nothing wrong with such practices and they may indeed be very helpful to people. But to exalt them into substitutes for inward purification is, as he puts it elsewhere, like cleaning the outside of a pot while leaving the inside filthy.

VII

LAST DAYS IN GALILEE

67 *Crumbs From God's Table*

MATTHEW 15.21-28   MARK 7.24-30

The dispute about exterior and interior cleanliness that we considered in the last section seems to mark, in the Evangelists' minds, the end of the public ministry of Jesus in Galilee. Jesus now travels north with his disciples to the borders of Tyre. We are asked to suppose that he wished to be alone with his disciples for a while, remaining so far as possible incognito to the rest of the world. A Gentile woman, however, recognizes him and begs him to cure her mentally deranged daughter.

Jesus, we are to understand, sees his mission as primarily to the Jews, his own people. He tells the woman that he must first take care of his own. No household would neglect the members of the family to feed the dogs first. At this the quick-witted woman points out that the dogs eat the crumbs that fall from their masters' table. Jesus likes that reply and tells the woman that her daughter is cured. The woman returns home and finds the girl in bed and well.

98

The symbolism here is impressive. Although it is true that we should not spread our energies thin, "casting pearls before pigs" as Jesus elsewhere puts it, neither should we hoard spiritual treasure for ourselves or for a narrow circle of people whom we take to be spiritually advanced. A bright child of ten may pick up what has eluded a sixteen-year-old dullard. Even a dog, when hungry, may profit more from a morsel that has slipped to the floor than does his well-fed master from what is on that table. All living beings are evolving, physically and spiritually, some more rapidly than others. Avarice with spiritual treasure is the worst possible kind of greed and has the most devastating results, withering our very roots.

68 *Ephphatha*

MATTHEW 15.29-31   MARK 7.31-37

From the region of Tyre, Jesus travels still farther north through Sidon and then south again to Decapolis, on the southeastern shore of the lake. A deaf man is brought to him, the man's speech impaired from the deafness. Taking the man aside, he communicates with him by signs, putting his finger into his ears and touching his tongue with saliva. Then Jesus looks upward, sighs, and says, "*Ephphatha.*" This is one of the very few places in the Gospels in which the Aramaic word is retained in the Evangelist's account. The word means "Be opened." The man, his ears being opened, begins to speak plainly.

This story provides a striking symbol of the basic principle of Jesus's teaching: openness. Evil, physical or spiritual, is always seen as some kind of shutting off. As a plant shut off from the sun and rain soon dies, so the spirit of a man or woman dies when it is shut off from the divine energy. If there is so much as a chink open to that health–giving energy the spirit may survive; if we are opened wide to it, our spirits will be restored and thrive. *Ephphatha* is the key command. The traditional matutinal office of the Church begins: *Domine, labia mea aperies:* O Lord, open thou my lips. If we coop up our spirits we die a spiritual death as surely as our bodies would wither if we retreated to a dark closet. When our spirits die, the death is reflected in our bodies, which are their instruments. A spiritually active man is open both to new ideas and to new people. A little girl, asked to define a saint, remembered the stained glass windows she had seen in church and replied, "A saint is a person who lets the light through." To be able to let the divine light pass into us and through us instead of blocking it is the hallmark of spiritual maturity. *Ephphatha:* be opened!

69 *No Sign Could Convince the Blind*
MATTHEW 15.39, 16.12   MARK 8.10-21   LUKE 12.54-59

The Pharisees and Sadducees keep on asking for a sign. Jesus reminds them that they can tell by the color of the sky what sort of weather is coming, yet they cannot discern the signs of the spiritual climate. No sign could convince them, so no sign shall be given them. He then leaves them and returns to his disciples.

Meanwhile, the disciples have forgotten to buy bread and their minds are on this neglect when Jesus warns them to beware of "the leaven of the Pharisees" and "the leaven of Herod." Naturally, they think he is alluding in some way to their not having obtained bread. Then Jesus asks them, "Don't you understand? Is your heart so hardened, are your eyes so blind, and your ears so deaf? Don't you remember the feeding of the crowds and how many baskets were left over?" Then the disciples perceived that he was speaking not of the leavening of the bread we eat as food for the body but of the leavening of the food for our souls. That is what is important above all else.

The word "leaven" (*zymē*) is used figuratively here and elsewhere in the new Testament to signify any pervasive influence, good or bad, but especially the bad. So "the leaven of the Pharisees" is their general attitude, through which they depreciate the value of all spirituality they touch. Jesus knew that his whole teaching, even his very presence, was all the sign needed. It was their inner blindness that made them seek outward proof of inward realities. He also alludes to "the leaven of Herod," by which he means a different method of evading spiritual realities: a retreat from them into worldliness, into mere conformity to the ways of the world. Even the disciples, Jesus complains, are insufficiently geared to spiritual realities; hence their excessive preoccupation with bread for eating.

70 The Blind Man at Bethsaida
MARK 8.22-26

At Bethsaida, on the east side of the lake, a blind man is brought to Jesus who, still seeking to avoid publicity, takes the man outside the village. He uses saliva as in the cure of the deaf man that we have just considered. Here, however, an interesting feature is reported by Mark, in whom alone this story is to be found. After the first application to the blind man's eyes, Jesus asks whether he can see. The man replies that he can see only shadows, men who look like tree stumps walking. Jesus then places his hands on the blind man again and this time the man sees clearly. Jesus tells him to go home, avoiding the village.

The story provides a symbol of the importance of privacy in such matters. Impostors need an enormous amount of publicity; people of genuine spirituality seek, rather, to avoid it, for they need no "signs" and know that if people cannot see spirituality at work no "sign" could possibly make any difference.

71 Peter Recognizes Jesus as the Messiah
MATTHEW 16.13-20   MARK 6.27-30   LUKE 9.18-21

Jesus goes on to Caesarea Philippi at the foot of Mount Hermon. Here, alone with the disciples, he asks them what people say about him. Who do they say he is? They tell him that some say he is Elijah returned to earth; others are saying that the spirit of John the Baptist has come into him; others again suggest that he is the reincarnation of one of the other prophets.

"But who do *you* say I am?" Jesus then asks. Peter, acting as spokesman for the others (the first time we see him coming into any such prominence) answers: "Thou art the Christ, the son of the living God." Jesus then felicitates Peter on his spiritual discernment. It is not something Peter could have learned from anyone. Only through his openness to divine truth could he have attained this esoteric knowledge.

Matthew alone adds the now famous words attributed to Jesus: "You are Peter" (*petros* represents the Aramaic *kepha*, a rock), "and on this rock I will build my Church." In mosaic on a frieze under the drum of the dome of the Basilica of St. Peter in Rome these words are inscribed in Latin in letters six feet high: *Tu es petrus et super hanc petram aedificabo ecclesiam meam.* For various not inconsiderable reasons many scholars have questioned the authenticity of this as an actual saying of Jesus, arguing that it has all the marks of an attribution made by the primitive Church. The question is not whether these were the exact words of Jesus, for whether we ever have the exact words of Jesus is doubtful. The question is, rather, did Jesus say anything like this or is it something that was added by ecclesiastical piety after his death?

I would suggest with Oscar Cullman and others that there is no definitive reason to reject it as a saying of Jesus. I would add, however, that there is every reason against interpreting it as the Roman Church has traditionally interpreted it. Rome has read into it an institutional and organizational significance rather than a spiritual one. It is one thing to say to a man called Rock, "Rock, what a rock you are! Your faith will be a solid foundation for the faith of all who learn divine truth through me." It is another and very different thing to establish on such words the vast institution, organized on typically Roman lines, that is the Roman Catholic Church today. Whatever claims may be made for it, none of them can have the words of Jesus to Peter as their basis.

Jesus ends by urging the disciples to keep the whole discussion secret. Let no one be told that he is the Christ, the promised Messiah, for in view of the common, materialistic and political understanding of the role of the Messiah in Jewish expectation, such a proclamation would lead only to further misunderstanding and abrasive and unprofitable caviling. The truth about his role in the divine scheme of things is to be seen as a hidden truth. It is esoteric knowledge not to be made available to the world at large. That would be indeed to have it "trampled underfoot."

72 Jesus Foretells His Tragic End and Final Victory
MATTHEW 16.21-28   MARK 8.31-9.1   LUKE 9.22-27

After Jesus has evoked the confession of his secret role in the divine economy, he tells his disciples what is going to happen. He is going to be sentenced to a cruel, violent death. It is *necessary*, he says, that he will suffer "many things," apparently aligning his forthcoming trials with those of the Suffering Servant in Isaiah 53. His suffering is to be the focus of the redemptive scheme that is to issue in the salvation of Israel.

Peter takes the words of Jesus here to be the expression of a sense of defeat and tries to encourage his Master. For this Jesus reproaches Peter as thinking along earthly lines, according to which such an end always spells failure. Peter wants to avoid such shame and disgrace, such anguish and such an ignominious death for his Master and such a failure for his Master's work. "It must not be," he says in effect. Jesus, however, sees Peter here as expressing the very spirit of the Evil One who had come to him in the wilderness when he fasted in preparation for his public ministry. No, this is the only way. He must suffer and die as he predicts.

Why? Because it is the very nature of divine Being to suffer. God suffers in the act of creating; that is, he empties himself, abdicates his power, lets his creatures be. So, then, Jesus must let the world have its way and take its course. Otherwise he could not accomplish the redemption of those who are to be called to participate in it. He could not lead humanity ahead in such a way as to give some the opportunity, the conditions necessary, for them to attain advancement to higher and higher levels of awareness in the spiritual realm. What is to happen to him is in line with the creative process itself, which is full of cruel suffering but ends in victory after victory for those who advance in spirituality. In full accord with this line of thought, he urges his disciples to recognize that they too must suffer. Everyone who tries to save himself will lose himself; those who are willing to lose themselves will save themselves. This is the paradox of the creation of spiritual values. There are no cosmic free lunches. No cross, no crown. No spirituality was ever attained or ever can be attained without suffering. That is why Jesus must and does regard Peter's outlook on the matter to be a travesty of the reality of the situation. So false is it that Jesus sees in it the very voice of the Evil One and says to Peter: "Get out of my sight, you Evil One." That is really the force of the Greek, *Hypage opisō mou, Satana.*

Finally Jesus predicts that in the end he will come with the angels of God to put things right. It is a prediction of the eventual spiritual triumph which the truly righteous are going to attain in the course of their evolution. Love and righteousness and truth shall prevail over the forces of materialism and the stupidities and wickedness of the willfully blind.

73 *The Transfiguration*
MATTHEW 17.1-13   MARK 9.2-13   LUKE 9.28-36

No story in the Gospels, not even the Resurrection accounts, is more full of esoteric, theosophical significance than the accounts found in all the Synoptics of the Transfiguration of Jesus Christ. All three relate it specifically to a date about a week after the conversations Jesus had with his disciples that we have just considered.

Jesus goes up a mountain to pray taking with him only three disciples: Peter, James, and John. When they have reached a place apart he is transfigured before their eyes. The three descriptions given by Matthew, Mark, and Luke concur in all significant details. His face radiates light and from his body an extraordinary white light is exuded, so bright that his clothes shine white, whiter than any cleaner could ever make them. Then Moses and Elijah appear, talking with Jesus. The onlooking disciples are amazed and fearful. (The presence of Moses and Elijah has a symbolic meaning, for as the former represented the Law, the latter was often taken as a symbol for the prophets.) Peter makes a seemingly clumsy proposal to build huts or grottoes for the three. This suggests that he is still struggling with his too materialistic understanding of spiritual truths, for what could be more childish than erecting buildings to enshrine spiritual realities?

The consciousness of Jesus (just disclosed to his disciples in revealing that his glory lay in his destiny to suffer humiliation and defeat and then after death to rise victoriously) was so intense that, as he prayed, it broke through the physical veil, irradiating his body and even his clothes. The three disciples (the same three whom he chose for his healing of Jairus's daughter and also in the Garden of Gethsemane on the eve of the Crucifixion) were chosen to witness the close connection between the spiritual realm and the physical, to see the power that the former has over the latter.

They hear a voice out of a cloud saying, ''This is my beloved Son.'' Then suddenly the transfiguration is over and Jesus is there alone. The brilliant light of Christ's spirit penetrates the physical flesh for only a short time; then it is over and everything looks as it was before the extraordinary vision. One remembers (Exodus 34.29) that when Moses came down from the mountain the people noted that his face shone. Here the light transforms both the face of Jesus and his whole body.

The disciples, having been solemnly enjoined to say nothing of what they had seen until Jesus should rise from the dead, ask about Elijah, for the scribes say that he must come before the Messiah comes. Jesus tells them that they are right to expect the coming of Elijah first; but, he tells them, Elijah *has* already come. Then, according to Matthew, the disciples know that he is referring to John the Baptist. There seems no doubt that Jesus is asserting the rebirth of Elijah in John the Baptist. And as the world treated John, so the world is to treat Jesus, who is even now preparing himself for the terrible ordeal he sees in store for himself.

74 Jesus Cures an Epileptic Boy
MATTHEW 17.14-20 MARK 9.14-29 LUKE 9.37-43

A man approaches Jesus begging him to cure his son who suffers from an epilepsy so severe that during a fit he falls sometimes into the fire, sometimes into water, foaming at the mouth and grinding his teeth. "If you can," the man pleads, "have compassion and help us." Jesus responds by saying that there is no question of "if"; healing is always possible when there is authentic belief. At this the man cries, "I do have faith. Help the little faith I have." Then after a final struggle in the epileptic boy, the fit is over and the boy lies as if dead; but Jesus takes him by the hand and the boy gets up, cured.

Later, the disciples ask Jesus privately why *they* could not have cured this boy, for had not they received the power of healing from Jesus? (See section 61.) Jesus, however, explains to them that this particular kind of evil affliction can be cured only through intense prayer. The power of prayer is incalculable.

75 Jesus Again Foretells His Fate
MATTHEW 17.22-23 MARK 9.30-32 LUKE 9.43-45

Again Jesus warns the disciples of what is to happen to him, telling them they must let his warning sink into their minds. But they still do not grasp the full meaning of his prophecy and they are afraid to ask him about it.

76 The Shekel in the Fish's Mouth
MATTHEW 17.24-27

For the upkeep of the Temple a tax was levied of half a shekel per person. When Jesus and his disciples had reached Capernaum, collectors came to Peter. "Doesn't your Master pay the half shekel?" Peter replied that they did, then went into the house to get the money. Before he could speak, however, Jesus asked Peter for his opinion: "From whom do earthly rules take toll or tribute—from foreigners or from their own sons?" Peter replied, "Foreigners." Then Jesus said: "Well, then, the sons are exempt." But he went on to say that nevertheless, so as not to cause ill-feeling, he must go to the lake, cast a hook, and in the mouth of the first fish that bites he will find a shekel to give to the collectors for the two of them.

In this strange story we get a glimpse of the attitude of Jesus toward the affairs of this world. It is, in short, that spiritual people, although they ought not to be embroiled in this world's affairs, should not ignore the demands the world makes. We are not to make enemies of the world's agents under the pretext of the higher loyalties to which we owe allegiance. Rather than make a great fuss about such things, go along whenever possible. There is no point in diverting energy from important spiritual enterprises to futile haggling with tax collectors and other bureaucrats, for that game is not worth the candle. What are a few shekels compared to the riches of "the kingdom of heaven"?

77   Childlike Purity and Forgiveness
MATTHEW 18   MARK 9.33-50   LUKE 9.46-50

The disciples ask what seems indeed a rather childish question: "Who is greatest in the kingdom of heaven?" Jesus, in reply, calls a little child, puts the child in front of them, and tells them that unless they become as open and loving and forgiving as a little child, they will not be ready to enter into the kingdom of heaven. Whoever makes himself smallest will be greatest in the kingdom of heaven. Rather than finding yourself in the odious position of putting obstacles in the way of those struggling below you in the scale of evolutionary development, cut off the hand or the foot that is the cause of your standing in the way. Whatever you do, do not despise one of the "little ones." The angels that specially guard them are close to the presence of God.

He follows up with a similar line of thought. Suppose a shepherd has a hundred sheep and one of them strays. Won't he leave the rest and go after the one mettlesome sheep that has left the fold? Of course! The sheep that has strayed is of special importance to God.

So powerful is prayer, the mightiest form of energy that can be generated by a human being, that if two agree to ask anything at all, the prayer will be great in the sight of God. For where even two or three are together in Christ's name, he will be there with them and their prayer shall be effective. This saying does not diminish the power of solitary prayer but it does support the practice of inviting others to pray for a particular end in which they, too, have a concern. When many pray together with great faith in their hearts, a tremendous spiritual energy is unleashed. Prayers are not answered like a letter to one's councilman or senator; *they produce an effect*, just as, in the physical world, does a boiling kettle. Not only is there thought transference, the energies of those engaged in such prayer are hooked up to the divine source of all energy.

The conversation then turns to forgiveness. Jesus, talking again of the kingdom of heaven, tells the parable of the wicked servant whose master, in response to his pleas, forgave him a huge debt. The man then went forth, put pressure on a fellow servant who owed him a few dollars and, when the latter could not pay, threw him in prison. The master, hearing of this monstrous ingratitude, sent for the servant whose debt he had forgiven and exacted from him the full penalty of the law. That, said Jesus, is how things work in the kingdom of heaven. In that spiritual dimension the moral law operates inexorably. Love, however, conquers all and gratitude is one of the fruits of love. When love is extended to those who are undeserving and ungrateful, its priceless treasure is withdrawn from them and they must face the process of laboriously working their way out of the enormous moral debt they have incurred. Love, compassion, forgiveness are not always easy to give, but for the unloving they are even more difficult to receive. Only loving hearts know how to accept love, the great inner mystery of the spiritual realm, that "kingdom" where God is King.

Peter asks Jesus to what extent, then, are we to forgive: "Seven times?" Jesus answers: "No, seventy times seven." That is to say, "umpteen" times, innumerable times, for love is not equipped with a pocket calculator. Love does not even understand the meaning of "how much." Nor can the value of love be grasped till we first understand the price of a karmic debt, which may take trillions of years to repay, but which love can cancel with a stroke of the pen if only the recipient is loving enough to accept it.

78 *The Feast of Tabernacles*

JOHN 7.1-52

The Feast of Tabernacles is, along with the Passover and Pentecost, one of the great celebrations in the Jewish calendar. All Jews who could possibly make the pilgrimage to Jerusalem to attend it were expected to do so. Jesus knew, however, that there were people in Jerusalem who wished to destroy him. When, therefore, the disciples propose that they all go to Jerusalem so that the people might see the works he does, Jesus demurs.

They point out that a man who wants to have his works known must go out and meet people and let them all see what he is doing. Jesus replies that it is all right for the disciples to go, for the world does not hate them. It is he who is hated, because he has shown the world how evil it is and the world does not like that. So, then, Jesus tells the disciples to go up themselves and let him stay behind in Galilee.

Nevertheless, after the disciples had gone up to Jerusalem, Jesus follows incognito. He is recognized, however, and some stand in groups whispering about him. Some are of the opinion that he is a good man, but they are afraid to say so very openly. The Gospels abound with allusions to this aspect of human wickedness: many individuals would do right and maintain justice if left to themselves, but they are too cowardly to stand up for what they know perfectly well is right. Lack of courage likewise disposes people to judge by appearances, for they dare not look to the reality behind.

The Feast of Tabernacles would last eight days. Probably on about the fourth or fifth day, Jesus apparently changes his mind and teaches in the Temple, presumably because, since he had been so widely recognized, there was no longer any point in his trying to pass unnoticed. Some of the pilgrims who knew of his early years wonder aloud how he learned to read, since he could not have been taught. (One must bear in mind that literacy in those days was an unusual accomplishment, an art peculiar to certain walks of life, not at all a widespread ability.) Jesus tells them that he did not teach himself how to read; his ability to do so comes from "the One who sent me." Others, inhabitants of Jerusalem, express astonishment that he is allowed to speak in the Temple, for they have heard that the authorities want to destroy him. They say they know very well where this Jesus comes from, but nobody knows when the Messiah is to come. Jesus, teaching in the Temple, tells them: "Yes, you know me and you know where I came from." He goes on to affirm that he has not come of himself. He has been sent by the divine One, whom he knows and whom they, his accusers, do not know.

At this, some are of a mind to have him arrested there and then. The priestly hierarchy is watching him. The Temple police are sent for. Apparently because of lack of unanimity among the crowds, he is not arrested. He warns his hearers that he will be with them a little longer but after that he will go whither they cannot find him, meaning that he will enter into the spiritual realm to which they have no access, being what they are. His enemies do not understand this. They surmise, in their mean and narrow way, that, having failed with his own folk in the Palestinian homeland, he may be taking off to see what impression he can make on the Jews dispersed throughout the Mediterranean lands. That would be a way of making a name for himself among the Gentiles. So hidebound are they in their prejudices that there is no conceivable way in which they could be led even to entertain the possibility that Jesus's words might be worthy of an attentive ear.

Nicodemus happens to be among the crowds and he remonstrates with them. Surely, he says, the Law does not allow judgment to be passed on a man without a hearing? But the crowd is in no mood for reason and jeers sarcastically at him saying he must be another Galilean, upholding his friend with some sort of local patriotism. If he will look at the Scripture, they tell him, he will see that no prophet ever comes out of Galilee.

79 The Woman Caught in Adultery
LUKE 7.53-8.11

This passage, although found in modern Bibles, is not in any of the most ancient Greek manuscripts, with the exception of the Codex Bezae. Most of the early Fathers did not include it in the Gospel according to John. Some Greek manuscripts attach it to Luke 21.37. Although we may take the story as pertaining to a venerable tradition, it is extremely unlikely that it was ever part of John's Gospel. The style is very unlike John's. Certainly it is out of place where it now occurs. It is nevertheless a beautiful story.

According to the Torah, the punishment for adultery was death by stoning. Jesus is asked what he thinks should be done. After writing on the ground with his finger (the only instance on record of his having written anything), he suggests with characteristic acuity that in his judgment the woman should be stoned to death and the stoning should be begun by a sexually guiltless man. One by one, the men leave in order of precedence, that is, the eldest first, until at last only Jesus is left.

"Where is everybody?" Jesus asks the woman. "Hasn't anybody condemned you?" The woman answers, "No one, Sir."

"Neither do I," says Jesus. "Now go away and don't sin any more."

The story brings out very dramatically the relation Jesus sees between the Law and the Good News he is preaching. He upholds the Law. Adultery is an abomination and Moses was right to conserve social mores by legislating a very drastic punishment for it. Nevertheless, there are sins much worse than sins of the flesh which are, moreover, so common that when it comes to executing punishment for them, the judge who orders it must be a very unusual man or else a cruel hypocrite. So mercy prevails over justice and Jesus sends the woman away with an admonition. The story provides a paradigm of how divine love strengthens us by forgiving us. Forgiveness, when we know how to accept it, is a tremendous source of strength.

80 *The Light of the World*

JOHN 8.12-30

Jesus, speaking to the people in the Temple treasury, declares himself "the light of the world." To follow him is to have "the light of life." The light results from the possession of life eternal. Jesus's words here echo the prologue with which our study began, in which Jesus is identified with the Logos who brings into being all living entities and whose life can become the light of men.

When the Pharisees chide Jesus for testifying in his own behalf, Jesus reminds them that the testimony of two witnesses is admissible. He has a witness: the Father who sent him. But they can know neither Jesus nor the Father because they are "from below."

The key message in the rest of the discussion is that Jesus makes available truth that bestows spiritual freedom. As the discussion proceeds, however, it becomes more and more acrimonious. When at length Jesus claims that "before Abraham ever was, I Am," they pick up stones to throw at him. Jesus, however, escapes them and leaves the Temple.

The light that Jesus bestows is visible only to those who are open to receive it. They have in fact been looking for it and have reached that point in their spiritual evolution at which they have become capable of seeing and understanding its import. They have been in one prison of the mind after another. Now they are like birds who have found their wings. No prison can ever again hold them. They have found the truth that confers upon them a hitherto unimaginable freedom.

VIII

FINAL TRAVELS

81 *The Calling of the Seventy*

MATTHEW 19.1-2, 8.19-22, 11.20-30
MARK 10.1
LUKE 9.51-10.23

Jesus now sets out on a long journey in the general direction of Jerusalem, continuing his public ministry of teaching and healing in the course of his travels. A good many of his doings attributed to this period are reported by Luke alone.

Passing through Samaria, he sends messengers ahead to try to prepare a visit to a certain village. The villagers, however, seeing that he was bound for Jerusalem, will not receive him, for there was much bitterness, as we have seen, between the Samaritans and the Jews and prejudice was rife. The disciples James and John, indignant at this affront to their Master, propose to retaliate by invoking fire from heaven to destroy the inhospitable villagers. Jesus, however, rebukes them for this proposal and they all pass on to another village.

On their way they encounter a man on the road who

tells Jesus he will follow him anywhere. Jesus warns him that although foxes have holes and birds nests, he has nowhere to lay his head. Jesus invites another man to follow him and the man agrees but says he must first go to bury his father. To this Jesus replies, "Let the dead bury the dead." Apparently he means that the generality of people are spiritually dead and are therefore well-fitted to conduct funerals: an ironical allusion intended to call the man's attention to the conditions of discipleship. When we are engaged in the enterprise of creating spiritual life there is no time for even burial rites, which can be done just as well by anyone. A third man proposes to follow Jesus but wants first to say good-bye to his family. Jesus will not allow this, saying that nobody is any use for "the kingdom" who puts his hand to the plough and walks back. You can't plough a straight furrow walking backwards.

Jesus is now said to have commissioned seventy or seventy-two disciples. Whether this is to be taken literally is doubtful, to say the least. It is highly probable that about this time he would wish to add to the original appointment of twelve, and it is not at all remarkable that the original twelve retain prominence. But the number seventy is suspect, particularly since it was a sacred and symbolic number. In Genesis 10, for instance, it is given as the number of the nations on earth. The number, however, is no doubt unimportant. More interesting are the injunctions Jesus gives to the new recruits.

They are to go out two by two into the towns and villages that Jesus intends to visit. He is well aware of the pitfalls that lie in store for them. "I am sending you out like lambs among the wolves," he warns them. They are to carry only the clothes they wear—no purse, no haversack, no sandals. They are to salute nobody but go their way, bent on the business for which they have been appointed. They are to greet any householder whom they visit with a blessing on his house, eat whatever is offered them, and after healing the sick they are to teach that the kingdom of God is near to them.

The notion of the nearness of the spiritual realm, the kingdom of God, is peculiarly significant in the teaching of Jesus. This "kingdom" is said to be "within" us. Sayings attributed to Jesus, although not found in the Gospels, include such injunctions as "Lift the stone and you shall find me" and "Cleave the wood and I am there." These are words characteristic of teachers of the Ancient Wisdom. Between the "ungodly", unspiritual man and the divine power the distance is infinite. Seekers should remember that and keep their distance from God, as Moses knew when he held converse with him long ago.

When people become spiritually developed, however, they find the divine energy right at hand, even working within them. All the great mystics testify to that. Jesus also tells his disciples that if any household rejects them when they come in his name, that household will fare worse on the "day of reckoning" than even Sodom. Sodom had fewer advantages than are being now offered by Jesus through his disciples.

The new disciples return, reporting that even the demons obey them when they utter his name. Jesus tells them that he has seen Satan himself fall like a bolt of lightning from his high place in heaven. Whether he means that he was *present* when, according to ancient legend, Satan was thrown out of heaven, or whether he means that he was aware of the success of the disciples in coping with the devils, is not entirely clear. On the latter view the implications are interesting, since the remark plainly attests the extra-sensory perception Jesus claims.

He is keenly aware of what is going on in the spiritual world around him, for he belongs preeminently to that world. Nevertheless, he tells them that far more important than their success with the evil spirits is the fact that they are enrolled in the register of names "in heaven." They have made a leap in spiritual evolution.

After an ecstatic prayer, he goes on to tell them they are indeed to be congratulated, for many great kings and even prophets have longed to see what they are now seeing.

82 *The Good Samaritan*

LUKE 10.25-37

A lawyer asks Jesus what he must do to inherit the "eternal life" that Jesus keeps talking about. Jesus asks him what he finds by way of directions in the Torah. The lawyer somewhat conventionally quotes that all-sacred source (Deuteronomy 6.5 and Leviticus 19.18) to the effect that he must love God and his neighbor. Jesus highly approves the answer. The rule was well known. It summed up the Law. The second part of the summing up, the part about loving one's neighbor, is really a statement of the Golden Rule which, as we have seen (Section 44), was already rooted in the Hebrew tradition and expressed in the sacred writings of the Jews. The lawyer, however, presses Jesus for a definition of "neighbor." Jesus responds with a story.

A man was on his way from Jerusalem and fell into the hands of bandits who took everything he had and beat him up, leaving him bleeding and unconscious. A priest happened to pass by, then a Levite. Both saw the man lying there half-dead and both, in turn, passed by on the other side of the road. At last a Samaritan chanced to come by and, when he saw the victim, bandaged his wounds, lifted him on to his horse, and took him to an inn, telling the innkeeper to take care of the man. Further, the Samaritan said, if any expenses were incurred above the amount of money he was leaving for the man's care, the innkeeper would be paid back the following day when the Samaritan would stop on his way back.

Jesus then asked which of the three was a neighbor to the unfortunate victim of the robbery. Of course it had to be the Samaritan. Then Jesus, alluding to the lawyer's original question as well as his request for definition of "neighbor," told him to go and do the same.

This is probably the only context in which most Christians today ever hear of the Samaritans; yet the fact that the kind man was a Samaritan is central to the story. The Samaritans and the Jews had no dealings with each other.

Jesus himself was rebuffed by a Samaritan household and
his disciples were astonished when they found him talking to a Samaritan woman at the well. The last person on
earth, then, of whom a Jew would expect such neighborliness would be a Samaritan. It is almost as if a Hindu
were befriended by a Muslim. The definition the lawyer
asked for was not provided in a neat form such as one
might now find in a good dictionary. It pervades the
whole story, which dramatizes the meaning of the term
in such a way that the listener finds it ringing in his ears
as the story reaches its climax. Your neighbors are not
only the people who live on your street; nor are they even
the people in your home town; not even members of your
own nation or your own race or religion. Your neighbor is
anyone who needs your neighborliness. The definition
makes an enormous difference to the meaning of the
second part of the summing up of the Law.

The vividness of this story brings out the whole character of Jesus's message to humanity. It is not a new message. It is one very much ingrained into the treasury of the
Ancient Wisdom in which all the religions of the world in
one way or another participate. Whatever is distinctive
about the message of Jesus, it does not lie in his ethical
teaching.

83 Mary and Martha

LUKE 10.38-42

As Jesus and his disciples proceeded on their journey
they came to a village where a woman named Martha
invited them into her house. She has a sister called Mary,
who listened to Jesus while Martha attended to the household chores, getting the meal ready and serving it. Martha,
annoyed that her sister seems to be getting all the attention while she is working hard, urges Jesus to tell Mary to
come and help her with the serving. To this Jesus answers
that Mary is attending to the one thing needful above all
else: the spiritual life. This must not be taken away from
her. Martha was doing very well with her chores and Jesus

was not ungrateful; but he insisted on recognizing that Mary, who was sitting rapt in meditation at Jesus's feet, had chosen an even better part.

This beautiful story brings home the importance Jesus attached to the contemplation of spiritual truths. Nothing could replace them; nothing must be allowed to supersede them. How much this is in line with the Ancient Wisdom and the teaching of all the great mystics of every tradition in the world! How far removed it is from the outlook of those who see no value in Christianity except as a tool for the advancement of their socio-political theories! This is a profoundly spiritual passage illustrative of the true nature of the Christian Way and of its mystical implications. The institutional aspect of the Church is its mere shell; the social consequences a mere echo. The inner nature of Christianity lies hid within its saints and mystics on whom the Church must rely for the sustenance of her life.

84 *The Man Blind From Birth*

JOHN 9

When the disciples encountered a man blind from birth they asked Jesus for an explanation of the condition. Was this condition the result of his own sin or that of his parents? The question clearly implies that they envisioned two possible causes. On the one hand, the condition might be due to a genetic defect transmitted by his parents, perhaps a congenital disease or hereditary weakness, in which case one could say the fault lay with his parents. On the other hand, it might be due to himself, in which case they must have had in mind a reincarnationist doctrine, for since the man was born blind he could hardly have been said to have sinned personally in the womb. The only possible way in which he could be held responsible for his condition must relate to a previous existence, a former incarnation or incarnations in which he had built up for himself what is known in Indian philosophy as bad karma.

That the disciples should think along such lines is not at all surprising. Reincarnationist theories were very widespread in the Hellenic world. As we have seen, the thought of that world by the time of Jesus had very considerably affected the thought, literature, and religious life of even such a culturally isolated society as was Palestine. There are suggestions of it elsewhere in the Bible, for instance, in the idea of a reincarnation of Elijah, which we have already encountered, and in occasional other passages such as Jeremiah 1.5; Psalm 139.16; and Ephesians 1.4.

The situation has also a symbolic meaning, on which Jesus focuses attention. Before the Incarnation of the Logos the world had been in darkness; now the light is shining bright. Using this teaching as the principle behind his action, Jesus now makes a paste out of his saliva and the earth and smears it on the man's eyes. We have already more than once seen Jesus using similar treatment, which apparently accorded with a practice at the time, for Tacitus and others tell us of such prescriptions for ophthalmic ills. At any rate, Jesus, having thus sealed the man's unseeing eyes, then tells him to go and wash his face in the Pool of Siloam, whose waters were used in certain religious ceremonies. (Sacramental symbolism pervades many of the stories in the Gospels, especially John.) The man does so and goes home seeing.

When friends and neighbors find him with his sight restored they ask, "Surely this cannot be the blind beggar?" He tells them that it is indeed he, that it was "the man called Jesus" who did it, and he describes how.

As in so many other cases it was Sabbath when the cure was effected. The making of the paste would have been technically a violation of the Sabbath, so the Pharisees inquire closely into the whole proceeding. They check with the parents of the man who verify that it is their son, and that he was born blind and can now see. How, precisely, was it done? Because of their fear, however, the parents will not admit to knowing how he had been cured or who had effected the cure. Their son, they say, is of age, so he must speak for himself.

When the Pharisees question the man, they warn him that the man who opened his eyes is a sinner. They ask him again for full details of how Jesus is supposed to have cured him. The man, weary of all the examining and cross-examining, says with a touch of sarcasm: "I've told you already and you wouldn't listen. Can it be that you want to be his disciples?"

"*You* are his disciple," retort the examiners. "*We* are the disciples of Moses. We know Moses; we don't know this man—don't even know where he comes from," that is, his background and his credentials.

"That's odd," says the once-blind man. "He gave me sight and you don't know where he comes from! If this man were not from God he could not do wonders like this. How could he be a sinner as you say?"

Infuriated, they taunt him. "*You* are a sinner, born in misery and degradation. And you presume to teach *us*!" So saying, they expel him from the religious community.

Jesus, having heard of this, seeks the man out and asks him if he believes in "the Son of Man." This curious phrase (*bar nāšā* in Aramaic) is the subject of much scholarly controversy that need not concern us here. It is a messianic title that is found 82 times in the Gospels and never in the Epistles, perhaps because it is so Semitic in background that it would not have been understood by Gentile audiences. Jesus, who is often reported as using it of himself, plainly intends it to be understood by signifying the Messiah long awaited by the Jews. So when he asks the man this question about "the Son of Man," the latter replies with a question: "Where is he, Sir?" "You are looking at him," says Jesus. The man, reverently acknowledging the claim, makes obeisance before him. The Greek verb used is *proskyneō*, classically used to signify the *salām* one gives to a superior—a king or a god.

In the final verses devoted to this episode, Jesus speaks of spiritual blindness and the Pharisees ask, no doubt mockingly, "Surely you are not calling *us* blind?" To this Jesus's reply is stinging: "Blind? If you were merely blind you would have less to worry about. You would be ready to have your eyes opened. But you who are supposed to know better say you can see. Unlike this man who was born blind, you must remain in your blindness."

This whole passage, however, is more than a record of yet another of the wonders Jesus performed and more even than an indictment of the kind of prejudice and pride that Jesus always abhorred; it is also a parable of how the divine light shines in the darkness and how only those who have at least a little candle burning in their hearts can hope to see it and begin to grasp its incalculable significance for us and for our salvation. It reflects also the beautiful working out of the karmic law. The poor man was born blind, inheriting the result of misdeeds or wrong attitudes in a previous life or lives; but he was also reaping the reward of thoughts or actions that had prepared him for his extraordinary privilege in this life: to have his sight restored by Jesus, the Light of the world. We do indeed reap what we sow in the spiritual world as in agriculture; but God's ways of helping us to be in the end victorious are wonderful beyond our wildest dreams.

85 *The Good Shepherd*

JOHN 10.1-21

The image of the shepherd and his flock was already a familiar one to readers of the ancient Scriptures, being an obvious way of presenting to people in a pastoral society the relationship between the Creator and his creatures, between independent divine Being and dependent entities such as we. The shepherd leads his flock, takes care of them, marks them, knows each of them, and guides them into the sheepfold. The sheep know him too and obey his voice. If a stranger tries to get them to follow, they will not obey.

These were not new ideas to Jesus's hearers. What was new and startling was Jesus's implied claim. He says, "*I* am the shepherd." Whosoever instinctively follows him follows God.

Jesus here uses, however, two separate figures: not only is he the Shepherd, he is also the Door, the Way. Here he calls himself the Door (*hē thyra*); elsewhere (e.g., John 14.6) he calls himself the Way (*hē hodos*). Unlike the Pharisees who bolt their doors against those who have found spiritual health and freedom because they want to make a prison out of the Torah instead of a way to God, Jesus claims to be an open door. Yet it is open only to those who already know God, those who have already reached a state of consciousness in which awareness of the presence of divine Being is already possible.

In the Middle East, several shepherds will sometimes sit down together and chat, letting the sheep mix. Then, when it is time for the shepherds to go their separate ways, each shepherd will give his own special call and the sheep will separate into their respective groups. If there are stragglers who still wander around undecided which group to follow, the shepherd to whom they belong will call them each by name, for by an old custom many shepherds give their sheep pet names just as we call dogs Punch or Goldilocks or whatever. Jesus uses the shepherd figure to bring out the bond that exists in the spiritual world between the Master and those whom he leads into the realm of light and life and love.

There are other shepherds, some good, some bad; but Jesus alone is the door or gate into the sheepfold. The false shepherds may try as they will to mimic the voice of the good ones and their peculiar call, but they will never succeed with the sheep that belong to the sheepfold of Jesus. At most they can only delay the sheep from reaching home.

There is some textual evidence that the part of this passage suggesting such ideas may have been an editorial addition arising from the experience of the early Church with the false teachers and evil bishops who were already arising in the Church. While that is exegetically conjectural, the passage is none the less prophetically apposite.

The false shepherd is a thief and a robber bent on vandalism or worse. He will be the first to run away, leaving the sheep shepherdless as soon as he hears the approach of wolves, for he is a coward who "cares not for the sheep." The fit is uncannily neat.

Some of Jesus's hearers, amazed at the kind of claims he is making, say that he must be crazy, raving mad (*mainetai*); but others wonder how a madman could make a blind man see. Crazy people are destructive, not constructive. What could be more constructive than making a blind man see and doing the other marvelous healing acts Jesus has been doing?

86 *Tell Us Plainly* JOHN 10.22-42

It is the Feast of Dedication and in the wintertime. Jesus is walking up and down the portico of Solomon in the Temple. People gather around him and ask when he is going "to level with them" and tell them plainly who he claims to be.

Solomon's portico was a sort of cloister on the east side of the Temple area and would provide some protection against the winter cold. The Feast of Dedication (mentioned in Ezra 6.16) began about the middle of December and lasted eight days. It commemorated the reconsecration of the Temple by Judas Maccabaeus after it was profaned in 168 B.C. by Antiochus Epiphanes. It took place two or three months after the Feast of Tabernacles. (See section 78.)

When Jesus says "The Father and I are one," the people take up stones to throw at him, for what he is saying seems outrageous. To identify oneself with God was the ultimate blasphemy to the Semitic mind. The gulf between God and man was accounted infinite.

Jesus, who as we have seen is as ready with biting satire as ever was Socrates, says ironically, "I have done many good works. Do tell me for which of them you are going to stone me." The people reply that they are not stoning him for good works but for uttering blasphemy. Jesus is only a man, yet he claims to be God. What could be greater blasphemy than that?

Jesus knows the Scriptures and quotes the Psalmist (Psalm 82.6): "I said you too are gods, sons of the Most High, all of you." The Psalmist makes God address these words to judges and rulers. If they can be rightly called "gods" surely one who is sent by God must so participate in the divine Being that to call himself God's Son is by comparison a modest claim!

The true meaning of Jesus's claim comes out in the end when he says: "The Father is in me and I am in the Father." Such a concept, familiar to all in the esoteric tradition of the Ancient Wisdom, is incomprehensible to the carnal and literalistic minds of his adversaries, who want to arrest him there and then. Once again he eludes them and goes back to the region where John the Baptist had done his work. People there note that while John did no healing wonders, Jesus does. All that John predicted about Jesus seems to be coming true. Many believe.

Time, however, is running out. Influential people are beginning to fear Jesus and are setting their minds against him. Still, before the end he will do many marvels and continue his teaching.

87   Attack on the Pharisees and the Lawyers

LUKE 11.37-12.21

This passage consists chiefly of a bitter invective against the Pharisees, uttered at a Pharisee's table. It is followed, on another occasion, by a warning to people who are gathered to hear his teaching. He warns these against "the leaven" of the Pharisees, which is hypocrisy. Jesus includes the lawyers in his condemnation because they invent legal problems they never have to cope with themselves. Their whole purpose is to make life difficult for others and easy for themselves. So they are aligned with the Pharisees, who are always so concerned with outward appearance and have forgotten, if they ever knew, how to look at the inside—that is, the spiritual realities contained in the shell. Both of them, Pharisee and lawyer, steal "the key of knowledge" (*hē kleis tēs gnōseōs*). The charge is directed to representatives of the Jews, Jesus's own people. But it applies also to their counterparts in all societies, not least those unworthy leaders in the Christian Church who, with very similar motivations, fear scholarship and any thought that may lead to that inwardness that brings knowledge (*gnōsis*) of spiritual reality.

88 *Readiness*

LUKE 12.35-48

Dress for action, Jesus warns his disciples. They are at war with the world. No time for dreaming! The enemy may strike any moment. Judgment is coming. Let them take care that they are prepared, so conducting themselves as to bring spiritual victory, not spiritual defeat and remorse. The wise servant is always ready for action.

89 *Not Peace But a Sword*

LUKE 12.49-53

Jesus, predicting his final trial which he sees approaching, exclaims, "I have come to bring fire to the earth! I wish it were blazing already! I have an ordeal still to face." He then warns them against supposing that he is here to bring peace on earth. On the contrary, he is to bring division, even within families, setting father against son, daughter against mother, brother against brother, daughter-in-law against mother-in-law, and so forth.

Here is a clear announcement of the nature of spiritual progress. It does not always work in tow with smooth family relationship. For marriage, which is the basis of the family, is an institution rooted in carnal needs and carnal aspirations. True, it may be blessed by God and be also therefore—and often is—a great instrument of spiritual advancement for both parties and their progeny, the offspring of the marriage; but it is nevertheless rooted not only in carnal desires but in aims which, although good in themselves and even instruments of spiritual development, are not to be identified with the still higher demands of the life of the spirit.

So following the way of Jesus may involve separating oneself even from one's family, breaking with one's dearest friends on earth, with all the intense distress which that inevitably brings. For the enemy of the good is not always merely evil; the enemy of the good can be the best.

90   The Signs of the Times

LUKE 12.54-59

Preaching to the multitudes, Jesus again warns them of the signs of the times. They are as plain as are to shepherd or farmer the signs of impending storm. Spiritual discernment, however, takes spiritual vision and spiritual vision arises from spiritual awareness.

91   The Nature of the Karmic Law

LUKE 13.1-9

A story was reported about the sufferings of certain Galileans at the hands of Pilate and of eighteen persons on whom the tower at Siloam had fallen. (These allusions were apparently well known to everybody at the time, although we have no knowledge of them today.) Jesus points out that there is no necessary connection between the enormity of outward suffering and the wrongs that a person may have done. People tend to suppose, like Job's comforters, that great external sufferings in life must be in some way deserved. Jesus indicates that there is no commensurate relationship.

While it is a cardinal principle of the Ancient Wisdom that we reap what we sow and that wrongs do take their toll, the way in which the karmic principle works is by no means clear to the outward eye. A wicked man or woman may be reborn to great wealth, for example, or a saint to abject poverty or the inheritance of genetic disease. The working out of the karmic law depends on a vast variety of circumstances. Having a tower fall on you may not be the pleasantest way to die; yet it may be a far better fate and entail far less suffering than the years of loneliness and distress that another may endure in a comfortable palace and in circumstances that make him the envy of all. Do not judge even the working out of the karmic principle by mere appearance. The man born blind had not necessarily been an exceptional sinner to deserve to be so reincarnated. As we saw in the relevant section, he must have been somehow specially favored to have Jesus not only heal his blindness but lead him to spiritual truth.

Jesus warns his hearers, however, to repent. He tells them the parable of the fig tree. This tree was not bearing fruit, so its owner was planning to cut it down, but he gave it, so to speak, a year's reprieve. It was on trial during the period. So are we.

92 A Cripple Woman Healed on the Sabbath

LUKE 13.10-21

Once again Jesus was teaching in a synagogue on the Sabbath. A woman there had been miserable for eighteen years, bent double and unable to straighten herself. Jesus touched her and she straightened up and praised God for her cure. The president of the synagogue, however, rebuked Jesus for healing her on the Sabbath, pointing out that there are six other days to do such healings. He told the people to come during the week to get healed, not on the Sabbath. Jesus reminds him that even the most observant Jew, when his animal falls into a pit on the Sabbath, does not wait until the next day to pull it out. The crowd is delighted, knowing he is right.

93 *Will Only a Few Be Saved, Sir?*

LUKE 13.22-30

Jesus goes from village to village on his way to Jerusalem. A man asks him, "Sir, are only a few to be saved?" No doubt he felt that his faith would be strengthened if only the veil that hides the future from the present might be lifted for even a moment. Jesus, however, wishes to stress the moral urgency of the situation. He says in effect, "Don't risk your eternal future! Take the narrow path, which is the only safe one. Don't gamble!" Gambling in the spiritual realm is the worst kind of gambling. Many procrastinate. Many become smug. Take nothing for granted! Those who rely on their hereditary privileges, even their spiritual achievements, may be in for a shock. All depends on the individual and what he thinks and does. The people who appear to be "sure bets" for the Kingdom may come to grief; the ridiculously unlikely ones may be right up front in the Kingdom. Nothing will be accepted as a substitute for personal righteousness and sanctity and love.

94 *Jerusalem, Jerusalem, You That Kill the Prophets!*

LUKE 13.31-35

News comes to Jesus that Herod is plotting against him and that he should keep away from Jerusalem. Jesus, refusing to be intimidated, responds by saying, "Go and tell that fox that I am constantly at work healing." He adds with bitter irony, "It would never do for a prophet to be killed outside Jerusalem!"

Then follows his lament over his beloved city: "Jerusalem, Jerusalem, you that kill the prophets, you that stone those that are sent to you by God! How often have I longed to gather your children together as a hen gathers her chickens under her wings and you refused. All right then! Now your house is left to you. Yes, I promise you shall not see me till the time comes when you say: 'Bless-

ings on him who comes in the name of the Lord.'" (These
are the words traditionally uttered in the Mass after the
Sanctus and before the Canon.)

The lament is not only one of the most tragic in the
literature of humanity; it symbolizes the reception that
crowds everywhere give to truth they do not wish to hear.
People generally do not know their enemies from their
friends. They welcome the former and persecute the
latter.

95   *The Parable of the Banquet*

LUKE 14.1-24

Invited to a Pharisee's house for dinner, he saw a man
in front of him who had dropsy. He asked the others
present whether it would be all right to heal this man on
the Sabbath. They were silent and Jesus, taking hold of
the man, cured him and sent him away.

Then he told a story. He has noticed how everybody at
banquets pick out the best places. That you should never
do, he tells the guests. Take the lower places; then your
host will move you up. Everyone who pushes himself forward will be humbled; he who humbles himself will be
promoted. He also told his host: "When you give a dinner, don't invite your rich friends and neighbors. They
will invite you back and so you will be repaid. Spiritually
you will be back to square one. No, you should invite the
poor, the maimed, the lame, the blind. They have no way
of repaying you." Spiritual advantage lies there, for that
is how treasure is laid up in "the Kingdom," where the
outward does not count.

Finally, when one of the guests exclaimed, "Happy the
man who will be invited to dinner at the Kingdom," Jesus
told one of his greatest parables. He was apparently eager
to make the point that one may have a sentimental nos-
talgia for the Kingdom, the spiritual realm, and yet lack
any real resolve to get there. In his story, the invited
guests are confident that they are invited virtually by

right. They do expect to attend but at the last moment, when the servant comes announcing that all is ready, they excuse themselves. (Apparently this was a social maneuver in accordance with customary etiquette. It was somewhat as with us when, invited to a prestigious affair, we pretend to look up our calendar to make sure we are free when in fact we would not miss the occasion for the world.) The host in the parable, however, is so weary of the ceremonial refusals that he tells the servants to go out into the streets and lanes and fetch the poor and the cripples—*they* will not hesitate. Finally, when the servants, having done so, say there is still room, the host says, "Go out then and bring in the waifs and the strays—anybody at all." So the banquet is attended, not by those originally invited, but by others, the poor and forlorn, who will so much more appreciate it.

In spiritual affairs one must take nothing for granted. One is in a very privileged position. The smug man or woman will find his or her place taken by the most unlikely people who will move in, eager to enjoy the spiritual food that the unworthy have spurned. If we are too finicky, others will come along to take our place and we shall be left far behind. Jesus is inveighing especially against those who become cozy in their conventional religiosity. That is the path to spiritual death. Wise men will beware of such pitfalls and keep the light in them glowing so that they are not thus overtaken and supplanted.

96   *Discipleship Means Carrying the Cross*

LUKE 14.25-35

Jesus warns the crowds that the cost of following him is high. To be his disciple, not only must one be willing to detach oneself from possessions, from friends, even from family; one must be prepared to carry a cross. Perseverance is essential for success in the spiritual realm. His disciples are indeed the salt of the earth, but what if the salt loses its taste? What good is it then? People will simply throw it away.

Here is a terrible warning. The spiritual realm looks attractive to many people and for many reasons. But the road to it is very hard indeed, demanding constant vigilance and courage such as can come only by associating with those much further advanced than we. If you hope for spirituality, remember the cost. Do not undertake the pilgrimage lightly as though it were a walk round an art gallery or an evening at a concert!

97 *Two Great Parables of Divine Love*
LUKE 15.1-10

Luke here gathers together two of the greatest parables of Jesus: (1) The Lost Sheep, and (2) The Lost Coin. They are intended to show the nature of divine love, which lets nothing of value be lost and goes to the uttermost ends of the universe to retrieve and save it. A faithful shepherd will go far out of his way to find a sheep that has strayed, as a careful housewife who loses a silver coin will search the house diligently, sweeping every corner till she finds it. The shepherd does not say he has ninety-nine sheep safely in their pen, so why bother about the odd one that is missing; nor does the woman say she has nine other silver coins so the tenth does not matter. The missing sheep, the missing coin, becomes all-important. Such then is God's care for us.

98 *The Prodigal Son*
LUKE 15.11-32

A third parable of divine love, found only in Luke, is probably one of the two best known of the parables of Jesus. (The other, also peculiar to Luke, is of course the Good Samaritan. See Section 82.) A rich man has two sons, one of whom leaves home, leads a riotous, dissolute life, till he has spent all his money and is starving. At last, in his misery, he goes back home to beg forgiveness and to ask his father to let him work as a hired hand. Instead, his father sees him coming and tells the servants to bring the best clothes in the house for him to wear, and to kill the fatted calf so that they may celebrate the return of his son who had been taken for dead. When the elder brother arrives on the scene he is annoyed, protesting to his father that it is unfair to make such a fuss over his younger brother who has been so unworthy, while he—the elder brother—has been so faithful yet never received any special attention. The father then tells the elder brother that he has always been assured of his father's love, but his prodigal brother, having strayed, has no such assurance. So they should both give him a special welcome to celebrate his return home.

Our sympathy naturally goes out to the elder brother, who has obviously an excellent case. He has faithfully remained at home to serve his father and enhance the family fortunes. His father is well aware of his son's fidelity and of the merit of his complaint. Nevertheless, his heart is so full of joy at the return of his other son whom he had given up for lost that he wants to pour out a cornucopia to express that joy. So, the Evangelist asks, in effect: "If this is how a normal human father would behave in such circumstances, can we expect less of divine Being?" He represents Jesus as using the illustration to show the nature of divine Being. Although the karmic principle is working everywhere and is at the root of all things, it does not exclude the operation of mercy and grace. On the contrary, when we are overwhelmed by the burdens we have brought upon ourselves and see no way out but the weary process of reconstructing what we have destroyed, sometimes a door opens ushering in light in a new way. Such is the gratitude and love engendered by the vision of this opportunity that a flood of tearful remorse cleanses us, releasing us from the weight of our burden and letting us skip forward on our way. For such a loving response brings us at once into tune with divine Being whose heart beats forever with love for all. Yet even

divine Being cannot overcome in us the consequence of
our karmic debt unless and until we overcome it ourselves by the outpouring of our love, born from the most
profound spiritual anguish.

Spiritual values are not easily attained. They are certainly not attainable in any automatic way, as government servants proceed a notch up the scale of pay after so
many years of service. Spiritual attainment entails anguish and often a sense of alienation from the very source
of all good. The greatest saints and mystics have learned
that God is known even more through his absence than
through his presence. We appreciate water more in the
desert than by the side of Niagara. When we emerge from
a drought, even the slightest shower is refreshing and we
relish every drop of it. The divine Creator lets his creatures be so that they may grow great. When he sees one of
them turn wayward and bent on self-destruction, what
may we expect when the creature turns back, trying to
regain what he had almost destroyed? Of course God will
not only receive him with joy but will even give him
special guidance and care. Any careful gardener would do
the same for a plant he had given up as withered and that
suddenly showed signs of coming back to life. He would
"baby" it even more than the others.

99 *Two Parables of Warning* LUKE 16

The steward in one of these two stories is found to be
dishonest, and so his rich master resolves to fire him.
Astutely, the steward hastily calls his master's debtors
and lets them off with much less than the full amount of
their debt. The master, on discovering this, admires the
man for his shrewdness in what we should nowadays call
public relations. He is fired from his position of trust, but
he has made sure of friends when he has no job. A neat
trick!

Jesus goes on to tell his hearers they should use money
to win themselves friends. Money is a tainted thing, a

little thing compared with the treasures of the spirit; but better use it well than ill. If you use it dishonestly how do you expect to be entrusted with spiritual riches? If you cannot be trusted in little things, nobody is going to trust you in big ones. The steward appeared to be a "good business man."

Jesus concludes, however, that it is impossible to be at the same time truly faithful in the service of God and in the service of money. The Pharisees, who love money, laugh at him for this and he tells them that they are the very ones who look virtuous to the world but are loathsome in the sight of God.

The story of Lazarus and the rich man is of a very different sort. Poor Lazarus was indeed a miserable fellow, in abject poverty and his body badly ulcerated. Even the dogs came to lick his sores. He died and was carried by angels to "Abraham's bosom." The rich man outside whose house Lazarus had lain fared sumptuously and wore the finest clothes. Eventually he died too and went instead to hell. From the burning flames he calls to Abraham to send Lazarus to him to bring him just one drop of water to cool his tongue. Abraham, however, points out that he had enjoyed all the good things of life while Lazarus had suffered the bad; now the situation is reversed. The rich man begs Abraham to do at least this much: to tell his five brothers about him so that they too do not come to suffer as he is suffering. Abraham then reminds the rich man that they have Moses and the prophets. Let them listen to them. The man replies that of course they won't listen to Moses or the prophets, but if somebody were to rise from the dead and warn them, they would listen. Abraham retorts, "If they won't listen to Moses or the prophets they won't be convinced even if one should rise from the dead."

The whole story expresses the karmic principle, couched in a local idiom and employing a scenario out of the religious imagery of the time and place. The message is provided in Abraham's final words, which express a terrible truth about humanity. When people close their minds to an important religious truth, there is no conceivable way of opening them. Prejudice so enslaves the mind that the one who harbors it will go to any lengths to preserve the prejudice that stands in the way of his facing the realities of the spiritual life. He will readjust everything to safeguard his precious prejudice. Heal all the lepers in the world; he will say it is an ingenious trick. If he has made up his mind, for one reason or another, to account you an impostor, there is absolutely nothing you can do to change his mind. In the spiritual realm this is especially disastrous, because advancement here depends so much on a constant rearrangement of our ideas and a willingness to keep our minds open to all sorts of possibilities. The spiritual realm, the "Kingdom," as Jesus calls it, is the realm of creativity *par excellence*.

On Luke 16.18, see Section 107 (Divorce).

100   *On Leading Others Astray*

LUKE 17.1-4

Jesus also warns against putting obstacles in the way of others. To wrong others is bad enough but to throw a monkey wrench in your brother's efforts to reach the "Kingdom" is the vilest of all injuries. Jesus refers to "these little ones." These are people who are less advanced in spirituality than we and who are therefore very vulnerable to discouragement and susceptible to being misled. To hinder anyone who is truly seeking the "Kingdom" is a sin that will bring terrible consequences on its perpetrator, who will be hindering himself far more than the seeker whom he hinders.

101   *Increase Our Faith!*

LUKE 17.5-6

The disciples ask Jesus to increase their faith. Jesus uses one of his favorite figures—the mustard seed. It is very tiny but grows very large. If only they had that tiny bit of faith, like the mustard seed, it would soon grow. We don't need to ask for increase in faith, for faith grows easily once the seed is well planted. First, however, we must see that it is well planted in the soul. No use putting it in a box or a drawer. Plant it well and you will never need to ask for an increase.

102   The Raising of Lazarus

JOHN 11.1-44

Lazarus is identified by the Evangelist as the brother of Mary and Martha. He also tells us that the family is of Bethany, a village on the south-east slope of Mount Olivet, about two miles from Jerusalem. It is not to be confused with another village called Bethany in John 1.28. News comes to Jesus that Lazarus, whom he loves very much, is ill.

The story that follows is one that has presented scholars with serious difficulties. Jesus, being with his disciples in Peraea, does not hasten to Bethany, in Judaea, to help the family he so much loves. Instead, he stays on for two days before saying to the disciples, "Let us go back to Judaea." They remind him that he has been almost stoned to death there; but he tells them that he must work while it is daytime, that is, while God still provides the opportunity. Then he adds: "Our friend Lazarus is resting. I am going to wake him." The disciples suggest that if he is resting—asleep—he will probably get well, since sleep is a panacea. The Evangelist interprets Jesus's words as a euphemism for "he is dead," and tells us that Jesus then speaks plainly, saying, "He is dead."

After two days had elapsed, Jesus could have known of the condition of Lazarus only by some form of what we now call extra-sensory perception. He had not been told by the messenger that Lazarus was dead but that he was ill (*asthenai*). According to John, he now says first that Lazarus is resting, then that he is dead.

If, however, we see Jesus as using extra-sensory perception we may go on to suggest that Jesus sees exactly what has happened. Lazarus was so weak that life seemed to have left him. His friends, taking him for dead, had buried him in a tomb, which had a boulder not on top but in front, to keep out wild beasts. Jesus has resolved to restore him, knowing that people from Jerusalem will be there and will have an opportunity of witnessing the wonder he is to perform.

When they arrive they find that Lazarus has been in the tomb for four days. The journey might well have taken as long as that, in which case the man would have been buried about the time of Jesus's resolve to go to him. The custom was to bury the dead almost immediately: a custom that would make entombment before death a very real possibility, since tests to determine whether death had occurred would be very primitive by our standards. A person might well lie in such a tomb, perhaps in a cave (with plenty of air coming in through the opening that would be covered only by a makeshift boulder), alive for several days though in a state of extreme weakness.

Martha, coming to meet Jesus, greets him with both a *soupçon* of reproach ("If you had been here my brother would not have died.") and an expression of faith: "I know that, even now, whatever you ask of God, he will grant you." Jesus replies, "Your brother will rise again." Martha takes this to mean the resurrection and says, in effect, that of course she knows he will eventually participate in the resurrection of the just on the "Last Day"; but this hope cannot assuage her present grief, nor that of her sister Mary, who is in the house weeping. Jesus replies, "*I* am the resurrection."

Martha then goes to fetch her sister, who throws herself at Jesus's feet and sobs out the same words of anguish that Martha used—if only Jesus had been there, this would not have happened. Jesus, distressed by Mary's wailing, asks where they have put Lazarus and they say, "Come and see, Sir." Jesus at this point bursts into tears (*edrakrysen ho Iēsous*). Some of the bystanders remark that since Jesus cured blindness, could not he have prevented Lazarus's death? Jesus then goes to the tomb and asks that the boulder be removed. Martha, characteristically practical, reminds Jesus that her brother has been dead for four days and so by now will be already putrefying, but Jesus reminds her of his promise to let them all see the glory of God in action. So they take away the boulder. Then Jesus, lifting up his eyes, prays, thanking God *for having already listened to him.* The implication is that what he has sought to happen has already occurred. Having finished his short prayer, he then says in a loud voice, "Lazarus, here! Come out!" And Lazarus, who has been partly bandaged according to custom, "comes out," which probably means that he rolls out, since the bandages would inhibit movement. Jesus then orders that the bandages be taken off to set Lazarus free.

Mighty indeed is the wonder Jesus has performed! From the moment he was told of Lazarus's illness he has been in psychic control of the whole situation, keeping Lazarus in life, despite the latter's great physical weakness. No story in the Gospels of Jesus's wonderworking is of greater parapsychological interest. He gathers up the intense love that the two sisters have for their brother, unites it with his own love, and uses it all in his final appropriation of the divine energy to restore the quiescent, almost-dead Lazarus to life. But for his unique perception into the psychic realm, Lazarus, having been taken for dead and treated for dead, would have died as no doubt many others in such circumstances have died after burial.

103   *Jesus Flees to Ephraim*

JOHN 11.45-54

Many of the people who witnessed these doings believed in him. But some reported them to the Pharisees, who held a meeting to consider what they must do. It was now plain that if Jesus were not stopped the whole Jewish nation would follow him and that might very well pro-

voke the vengeance of the Roman authorities. Something
of the kind had happened before, after the Judaean war.
They are naturally afraid that the privileges they enjoy as
a people within the Empire will be withdrawn. Caiaphas
points out that the solution is obvious: surely it is better
for one man to die than that the whole nation should be
destroyed! Jesus must be killed. So indeed the meeting
resolves.

Jesus, we are told, "no longer went openly among the
Jews, but left the district for a town called Ephraim, in the
country bordering on the desert, and stayed there with the
disciples." But if the meeting of the Jewish authorities
were private, as surely it must have been, how could Jesus
have learned of the resolution to kill him? Who would tell
him? Yet it is made clear that it was on that account that
he went into hiding. Again the implication must surely be
that he knew by extra-sensory perception.

104   *The Ten Lepers*   LUKE 17.11-19

While Jesus and his disciples were traveling, ten lepers
called to Jesus, begging to be healed. Jesus tells them to go
and show themselves to the priest. It is to be presumed
that they were healed on the way, for one returned to
Jesus to thank him and it turned out that this one was a
Samaritan. "Where are the others?" asks Jesus. "Were
not ten cured?" The only one to come back to give thanks
was a "foreigner."

105   *The Kingdom is Within You*

LUKE 17.20-18.8

The Pharisees ask when the Kingdom of which Jesus
speaks is to come. Jesus replies that it is not a Kingdom
that can be seen. It is *"within you (entos hymōn)."* It is
the spiritual dimension that he is talking about, of course,
not an earthly kingdom. It is there inside us, ready for us
to take possession, if we know how.

He also goes on to foretell what is going to happen. Justice, though slow in coming, will be done. He urges his disciples to pray continually and not to lose heart. He tells a parable about a widow who keeps pestering an unworthy judge for justice, and the judge at last decides he had better give it to her after all. If even such a judge can be prevailed upon to give justice, surely God will see that justice is done. Justice, under the karmic principle, is always done in the long run, however slowly the mills of God may take to grind.

106   *The Pharisee and the Tax Collector*
LUKE 18.9-14

The "publicans" mentioned in the Gospels were agents of the imperial government engaged in the business of collecting certain taxes. They were universally unpopular. No doubt many were dishonest, for the system tended to promote dishonesty and extortion. In the minds of most people the publicans symbolized all who deserve to be ostracized. Jesus, however, had no hesitation about consorting with publicans, even dining with them.

Here he tells the story of two men who went to the Temple to pray, one a Pharisee, the other a publican. The Pharisee gave thanks to God for the fact that he was a good man, just and fair, not a crook like these publicans. He fasted, he tithed; in short, he was a model of Jewish rectitude. That was indeed what had brought him to the Temple—to give thanks to God for his finding himself in such a satisfactory state. The publican, by contrast, could find nothing good to say about himself. All he could do was to beat his breast and confess that he was a poor, miserable sinner. Which went home in the healthier spiritual condition? The publican, of course. As Jesus's own mother Mary had exclaimed in the course of her rejoicing at the news brought her by the angel Gabriel, God puts down the proud and exalts the humble. The publican's genuine humble confession of unworthiness was worth far more than the Pharisee's righteousness.

107 *Divorce* MATTHEW 19.3-12 MARK 10.2-12

The regulations about divorce in the Torah are not unambiguous. Moreover, we have no means of knowing how common was divorce in Hebrew societies at various periods of history. The prophet Malachi rebukes those who leave the wives they had married in their youth (Malachi 2.14-15). According to Deuteronomy 24.1, a man who divorces his wife must certify it in writing. What constitutes grounds, however, is not clear. Moses could not well have accounted adultery a basic ground, for so severe was the law against adultery that the adulterous spouse was condemned to death, and therefore the question of divorce could not arise when the guilty party had been executed!

In Semitic countries only the man could institute divorce; but Roman law permitted a woman to institute proceedings. Although the teaching of Jesus throughout the Gospels is not entirely unambiguous on this subject and gives rise to controversy, it is clear that he thoroughly deplores divorce. So when some Pharisees try to corner him on the subject, asking him whether it could *ever* be lawful for a man to divorce his wife, he replies that it cannot be, since through marriage the man and woman have become "one body." So then, "what God has united man must not divide."

The Pharisees then ask, in effect, "Then why did Moses stipulate an instrument in writing in cases of divorce, if it were never to be permitted?" Jesus retorts that Moses so ordered because "you are so unteachable." In other words, the Law does not go far enough. Ideally, divorce should never occur. (See Luke 16.18.)

The Pharisees must have had in mind a dispute between two rabbinical schools: Hillel, which allowed the husband to divorce his wife for many reasons, and Shammai, which held to far stricter conditions. Jesus no doubt recognized the trap the Pharisees were trying to set for him and in his reply transcended both the teachings of Hillel and those of Shammai by implicitly pointing out that both schools had lost sight of the extreme sanctity of marriage, which is therefore ideally indissoluble. Even where divorce is allowed, it is still contrary to the divine will for human beings and is therefore deeply injurious to the spiritual life of those involved.

108   Little Children and the Kingdom
MATTHEW 19.13-15   MARK 10.13-16   LUKE 18.15-17

Not only does Jesus rebuke the disciples for stopping the children from coming to him; not only does he say, "Let them come to me"; he adds that the Kingdom *belongs* to such as they. Unless you approach the spiritual dimension as does a little child you will never get there at all. So he takes the children in his arms and blesses them because they provide a model of the singleness of heart, the freedom from corruption, the openness of mind, without which nobody can hope to find the Kingdom.

109   What Shall I Do To Get Eternal Life?
MATTHEW 19.16-30   MARK 10.17-31   LUKE 18.18-30

The man who asked the question was rich and of considerable social standing, perhaps a magistrate or a member of a local sanhedrin. Jesus tells him he must know the commandments, his duties to his fellow man.

The rabbis generally held that it was possible to keep all God's commandments, that is, to live a perfect life. The man is therefore not making any extravagant claim or exhibiting any unseemly pride in answering that he has kept all these commandments since his youth. What else? Jesus approves of the response and says there is, however, one thing the seeker lacks. He should sell all his extensive possessions and give the proceeds to the poor, so that he may have spiritual treasures instead. According to

Mark's account, it was because Jesus loved the man's outlook, his rectitude, his earnestness, his openness, that he made this proposal to him. Jesus is no doubt thinking of how he is soon to go up to Jerusalem, and of how his disciples have forsaken all to follow him. Alas, the rich man could not go so far as that and went away sadly. Jesus had asked him to go beyond the Law in order to attain the kind of perfection that opens up the spiritual dimension.

Jesus afterwards remarks that it is easier for a camel to go through the eye of a needle than for a rich man to enter into the Kingdom of God. Here he was using a proverbial expression: one of those picturesque exaggerations we find in some common sayings. We might use similar sayings. For instance, we might say of something very difficult that it would be easier to drain the Atlantic with a spoon, or something of that sort. He means, simply, that it is inordinately difficult for a rich man or woman to have insight into the nature of the spiritual realm. Why? Attachment to worldly possessions is by no means necessarily wicked, but it can blind one to the treasures of the spirit. A rich person may love music and other aspects of a cultured life, but the attachment to his possessions tends to keep him narcissistic. He may even admire spirituality and those who practice it; but he is not living spiritually any more than a spectator at a football game is playing football. He is an onlooker. Nevertheless, adds Jesus, what seems impossible to us is possible with divine help. Otherwise, very few would be saved, since we all have attachments to earthly things, even though we may not be rich. Still, the principle holds: detachment from earthly encumbrances is of incalculable help to anyone bent on making spiritual progress.

Peter, listening to all this, reminds Jesus that they, his disciples, have left their homes and all they had in order to follow him. Jesus assures him that they will reap a vast return in spiritual capacity and joy even in this life, and that they will be on their way to the attainment of eternal life, that is, the immortality that Jesus is to make possible through his own resurrection.

110   *Impending Suffering and Crucifixion*

MATTHEW 20.17-19

MARK 10.32-34   LUKE 18.31-34

Although there are slight differences in the Synoptists' accounts of this prediction, they all report Jesus as warning the disciples in clear terms of what is soon to happen to their Master. Matthew and Luke mention that he is to be handed over to the Gentiles, that is, the Roman authorities, "foreigners", to be cruelly and ignominiously punished. All the Synoptics foretell his resurrection. Luke alone says they did not grasp the meaning of his words.

111   *The Nature of Religious Authority*

MATTHEW 20.20-28

MARK 10.35-45

The disciples James and John come to Jesus with a bold, not to say startling, request. They want to reserve places when Jesus comes into "his glory"—one at his right hand and the other at his left! Jesus, seeing that they do not yet understand the nature of the spiritual realm, tells them that they don't know what they are asking. Can they drink "the cup" that he is to drink? (He alludes to the sufferings he is to endure.) Yes, they say, they can. Jesus tells them that they too are to suffer, but what they are asking is still not his to give them. Places in the spiritual realm are not reserved as one might reserve a seat in the synagogue or at a dinner table.

The other disciples are annoyed at the request these two made. Jesus then teaches them the basic principle of religious authority. In worldly organizations those who rule have certain powers which they exercise, lording it over those under their command. The higher they are in the system, the more power is vested in them, and therefore the more they wield. In the religious community, however, the situation is entirely different. The way to greatness and the spiritual authority that goes with it is not by the acquisition of power but by service. If anyone is to be first in the religious community he must be the servant of all.

How little understood is this fundamental principle! The service suitable to one who is to be a genuine religious leader is nothing less than a self-emptying, an abdication of all selfishness, in the interest not merely of the community but of every other individual member of it. For the service is not corporate service such as government servants give to a nation or state; it is personal service demanding personal love and entailing the profound understanding that is impossible without that love. An army officer seeking promotion to get greater power or a politician seeking office for the same reason is not admirable, but the desire arises from a natural and understandable weakness in human nature. Ambition of this kind need not be altogether bad. It may be accompanied by the development of virtues that to some extent neutralize the power-hunger. By contrast, a bishop or other religious leader who seeks power of that kind is not merely exhibiting a regrettable human weakness; he is a monster. For he is guaranteeing a trail of destruction in everything he undertakes. He cannot fail to demolish the very values he has been designated to uphold.

The reason for this principle is rooted in the nature of divine Being itself. At the heart of God is an eternal self-emptying, an eternal abdication of power, an eternal self-sacrifice, so that all who catch even a glimpse of its glory must inevitably long to emulate it.

Jesus said elsewhere (Section 85) that the false shepherd who tries to lead the sheep by mimicking the authentic shepherd's call is a thief and a robber. But surely he who does so hoping for easy access to power is a coward as well. Leadership such as Jesus taught his disciples entails a radically different motivation, which, as we are to see, he was about to exhibit superlatively.

112 *The Blind Man at Jericho*

MATTHEW 20.29-34
MARK 10.46-52   LUKE 18.35-43

There is a slight discrepancy in the accounts of this incident. Matthew says it occurred when Jesus and the disciples were leaving Jericho and that there were *two* blind men. Mark and Luke both say there was one blind man and that they encountered him as they were approaching Jericho. Mark mentions his name and family—Bartimaeus, son of Timaeus.

The central focus is that the blind man is told that Jesus is passing by and shouts to him, "Jesus, Son of David, have pity on me." Jesus "stood still" and told the disciples to call him. The man, throwing off his cloak, jumps up and comes to Jesus, who asks him what he wants. The man cries, "Sir, let me see again." Jesus restores the man's sight, and the man follows him, praising God.

113 *The Conversion of Zacchaeus*

LUKE 19.1-10

Jericho lies about twenty-three miles northeast of Jerusalem. Jesus visits it as he was approaching Jerusalem for the last time. Three episodes are connected with the visit: (1) the cure of the blind man, which we have just considered; (2) the conversion of Zacchaeus; and (3) a great parable about the "Kingdom," designed to prepare the disciples to wait long for its realization.

Jericho was the center of much trade, being on the principal caravan route from the East to Judaea. Zacchaeus was a tax collector, but no mere agent or underling as are most of the members of that class that are mentioned in the Gospels. He is described as a "chief" publican or "senior" tax collector; that is, under the customary system he would have purchased the tax collection rights for the area and would have leased them to underlings. So, especially in such an important commercial center as

Jericho, he would be a rich man. No doubt he had heard
that Jesus, unlike the more conventional rabbis, did not
seem to mind consorting with widely ostracized people
such as those of his class. Wishing to see Jesus for himself
and being apparently a rather short man, he climbed a tree
to get a better view of him.

Jesus, we recall from Matthew 10.11, had told his disciples that when they came to any town, to make inquiries
about residents likely to be receptive to spiritual teaching. Jesus may have received word that Zacchaeus might
be such a person. Be that as it may, his extraordinary
powers of discernment led him at once to detect Zacchaeus
in the tree and, with clairvoyant insight, he perceives the
shyness and diffidence in the "poor little rich man" who
was so eager to see him that he had climbed a tree to do
so. Jesus, by the outgoingness of his advance, makes an
instant conquest: "Zacchaeus! Hurry! I'm coming to stay
at your house tonight!" Zacchaeus makes his way down
the tree and welcomes Jesus. Like many rich men, he had
few real friends and was apparently so delighted at Jesus's
unconditional acceptance of him that he welcomed him
with much emotion. Even as they were walking to his
house, he was telling Jesus that he planned to give half his
riches to the poor. Moreover, if he had cheated anybody,
he would repay four times as much as he had taken.

Meanwhile, people are shocked that a religious teacher
should be going to eat with a man whom their prejudices
excluded from their society. Surely a holy man should
know better than that. But Jesus calls Zacchaeus a true
son of Abraham. His spiritual cure has been instantane-
ous. This is exactly the kind of man Jesus has come to
talk with, for his mission, as he has often said before, is to
save the lost. His is the light shining in the darkness.

114 *Investing Spiritual Treasure*

LUKE 19.11-28

We now come to the third episode connected with the
Jericho visit. Jesus, seeing that his hearers assumed that
when he reached Jerusalem he would usher in the "King-

dom" there and then, told a story.

A rich ruler gave ten of his servants each a sum of money—a *mina*, equal to a hundred drachmas. We may say $100. He tells them to do the best they can with the money entrusted to them and he will return to see what they have done. On this return, the first said that he made $1000. Excellent! He was rewarded by being given charge of ten territories. The second had made $500, so he would be given charge of five territories. The third brought back the $100, which he had carefully wrapped in linen and kept safely for his master's return, for he was afraid to venture anything with it, knowing what an exacting man his master was. Not only is he severely rebuked for his lack of enterprise; the $100 is taken from him and given to the man with the $1,000.

In this story, Jesus is preparing his followers to be left soon to fend for themselves. In the realm of the spirit, as in business, there is no place for the person who hoards what he has, lacking the enterprise to do anything with such spiritual gifts as have been entrusted to him. We cannot always remain mere novices, receiving our keep from our teacher; we must go out and use our gifts. Then we must be prepared to incur risk. We must invest our treasure as we would invest any financial capital we have received. Spiritual treasure no less than money must be used to achieve some sort of growth. If we show ourselves incapable of doing anything worthwhile with the gifts we have received, how can we expect to be trusted again? But if we invest our treasure well, we will be entrusted with more. So "everyone who has will be given more; but from the man who has not, even what he has will be taken away."

Having so said, Jesus goes on to Jerusalem.

115   *Mary of Bethany Anoints Jesus*

MATTHEW 26.6-13   MARK 14.3-9
JOHN 11.55-12.11

Six days before the Passover, that central feast in the Jewish tradition, Jesus visits his friends in Bethany—

Mary, Martha, and Lazarus. At dinner Lazarus is among the persons reclining at the table with Jesus. Martha serves. According to John's account, Mary, the other sister, used a pound of expensive perfumed ointment on Jesus in a gesture of affection. There appears to be some confusion between this anointing and other accounts which seem to relate to quite different occasions. In Luke's account the woman is a harlot, usually identified as Mary Magdalene. In Matthew and Mark, the woman—unnamed—anoints Jesus's head with the precious ointment. In John, Mary (Martha's sister) anoints his feet. All three, however—Matthew, Mark, and John—relate a very significant story in connection with the loving gesture.

When the ointment is poured on Jesus, there is some murmuring at the extravagance. According to Mark and Matthew, the disciples generally engage in the murmurings; according to John it is initiated by Judas Iscariot. Judas, who is the treasurer of the group of twelve, asks pointedly why the ointment was not sold for three hundred denarii (about a day-laborer's wage for a whole year) and given to the poor. What a waste! John adds, however, that Judas did not really care for the poor but was a thief. He carried (*ebastazen*) the kitty and helped himself to the money in it. The implication, of course, is that he could have skimmed off a great deal of such a large sum as the ointment would have fetched. The Greek verb used for "carry" (*bastazō*), although it does mean "to carry around," means also "to carry off" or, as might be said today, "to rip off"—to steal.

All three Evangelists, however, agree in their report that Jesus praised the loving act, saying, "Let her alone! You always have the poor with you, but you will not always have me. This woman, her heart full of love, has done this for me and it is a good thing that she has done, for it is nothing less than an anointing for my burial." Matthew and Mark add that Jesus also predicted that wherever the Good News of the Kingdom would be preached all through the world, this story would be told and Mary commemorated in the telling of it.

It is a moving end to the story of Jesus before his final arrival in Jerusalem, the scene of his arrest and cruel execution.

IX

BETRAYAL, AGONY AND DEATH

116   *Jesus Enters Jerusalem on a Donkey*
MATTHEW 21.1-11   MARK 11.1-11
LUKE 19.29-44   JOHN 12.12-19

The road from Jericho to Jerusalem ran over arid country among limestone rocks, a symbol of the grim end approaching. When Jesus and his disciples are in sight of the Mount of Olives, he tells some of them to go to the village where they will find a young donkey tethered, one that has never been ridden. They are to untie it and bring it to him. If anybody should ask what they are doing they will reply that the Lord needs it. They do exactly as commanded. The donkey's owners do in fact ask what they are doing and the disciples reply as they have been instructed.

When the donkey has been brought to him and some of the disciples have thrown their cloaks on its back, Jesus sits on it and rides toward the city. As he does so, people begin to gather palm branches and throw them, along with their cloaks, on the road by way of homage. It is what one would do to a king. Then as the city comes into view at the crest of the road, the people following him—pilgrims going to Jerusalem for the feast—burst into song, shouting "Blessings on him who comes in the name of the Lord! Hosanna! Blessings on the coming Kingdom of our father David! Hosanna in the highest heavens!" In the crowd are some Pharisees who call on Jesus to control his disciples and the exuberance of the crowd which they account unseemly; but Jesus answers, "If they were to keep quiet, the stones would cry out!"

The story is natural yet full of vivid symbolism. Jesus knows of the existence and the location of the unbroken donkey. Plainly this must be through the extra-sensory perception he so habitually exhibits. The crowd, no doubt encouraged by the disciples, behaves naturally, singing a cry of welcome (from Psalm 118.25-26). Jesus accepts the acclamation as fulfillment of the messianic prophecy of Zechariah. It is all as if the secret of Jesus has at last come to light. The secret is that Jesus is the fulfillment of that prophecy (Zechariah 9.9).

> Rejoice, heart and soul, daughter of Zion!
> Shout with gladness, daughter of Jerusalem!
> See now, your king comes to you;
> he is victorious, he is triumphant,
> humble and riding on a donkey,
> on a colt, the foal of a donkey.
> He will banish chariots from Ephraim
> and horses from Jerusalem;
> the bow of war will be banished.
> He will proclaim peace for the nations,
> His empire shall stretch from sea to sea,
> from the River to the ends of the earth.

The whole incident is a symbol of the messianic occupation of Jerusalem, the hold city. Zechariah's prophecy gives rise in later Jewish thought to interesting interpretations. One rabbi in the third century of the Christian era, for example, contrasts it with the prophecy of Daniel 7.13. He remarks that when Israel is deserving, the Messiah comes as with the clouds of heaven in great splendor, but when Israel is not deserving he comes poor and riding on a donkey. Christian exegesis, however, has generally seen the entry into Jerusalem on an unbroken donkey as a symbol of the gentleness of Jesus in all his ministry and indeed of his whole life of self-emptying love. As he chose a stable for his birth, so he now chooses the lowly beast for his final entry into the holy city.

117 *Jesus Curses a Fig Tree*
MATTHEW 21.18-19   MARK 11.12-14, 20-25

In Mark and Matthew the story of the triumphal entry into Jerusalem is followed by a remarkable incident. According to Mark, when it was getting late Jesus leaves the city for the neighboring village of Bethany. The following day, on leaving Bethany, since he was hungry he looked at a fig tree that had leaves on it to see whether he might find fruit. Since figs do not come into season until about June and the incident occurs in April, the absence of figs was to be expected. Yet, finding nothing but leaves, Jesus curses the fig tree, saying to it, "*Mēketi eis ton aiōna ek sou mēdeis karpon phagoi,*" that is, "May nobody ever eat fruit from you again!" The position of the words in Greek and the use of the double negative make the curse emphatic.

A traditional explanation of this extraordinary story is that Jesus, on the point of engaging in a spiritual conflict in which the operative force was false pretense, found a tree guilty of the same fault (having leaves that suggest the presence of fruit but no fruit in fact). Using the fig tree as a symbol for hypocrites, he cursed all of them. It was a way of teaching his disciples.

Although Jesus indeed used the barren fig tree as a symbol, the lesson he taught may not have been quite so simple. The tremendously long process of spiritual evolution begins even in lower forms of life in which there is fierce competition for survival. Not only do big fish eat little fish by the billions daily, but as every gardener knows, plants too have a hard time surviving in the presence of competitors. Salvation is not to be taken for granted. It is an infinite blessing, as every deeply religious person knows. God does not bless indiscriminately, going around like a politician patting everyone in his constituency on the back. On the contrary, his blessing is infinitely meaningful. By no means do all attain the divine wisdom. Many are called but few chosen to be numbered among the wise. The barren fig tree is a symbol not only of a hypocritical world but of the multitude of entities that "fall by the wayside." If, after a myriad chances provided by a myriad rebirths, we remain obdurate in our pursuit of folly, there can be no justification for our survival.

Further light, moreover, is provided by the Evangelists themselves. They relate that on the day after Jesus cursed the fig tree it was found to have withered. When the disciples remark on the fact, Jesus repeats one of his favorite injunctions about the power of faith: with faith you can do anything. It is spiritual power, energy that comes directly from God, bestowing power over all entities, power to bless but also to curse. Frivolous use of such power will boomerang, cursing him who so abuses it. Nevertheless, through faith one may curse as well as bless.

We all know that plants respond to the kindly words of a sensitive gardener who loves them. If a person of such limited psychic powers can so affect a plant, what must not we expect of Jesus?

The episode is, however, a peculiarly difficult one to interpret.

118 Cleansing the Temple

MATTHEW 21.12-17
MARK 11.15-19   LUKE 19.45-48

The Synoptists repeat the story that John places at the outset of Jesus's ministry. (See Section 18.) Exegetes are divided on the chronology. John may not have accounted the time of occurrence important. The common witness of the Synoptists seems more likely to represent the correct chronology. Or, of course, the incident may have occurred more than once.

As an opening to the events of what Christians traditionally call Holy Week, the cleansing of the Temple certainly has dramatic force. Jesus deplored the traffic in animals required for the sacrifice. People found it more convenient to buy the animals at the Temple rather than elsewhere, for then they could be assured of meeting the standards demanded by the Temple authorities. This enabled worldly ecclesiastical groups to control the lucrative trade. The very people who should have been leading Israel in spirituality were cornering the market of a profitable business over which they were gaining a virtual monopoly. Notoriously, this is what happens in all religion: the merest hucksters hover around the fringes of spiritual activity, taking advantage of whatever profit can be made out of the ritual and ceremony that attend religious practice. They are parasites of the most contemptible kind, religion-mongers who make even great spiritual realities look vile to those who can see no further than the odious trade of these racketeers.

In the Temple the children go on crying out, "Hosanna to the son of David!" The Temple authorities, scandalized at this outburst, ask Jesus if he hears what they are saying. Jesus makes the eloquent response, "By the mouths of children, babes in arms, you have made sure of praise." (Compare the Book of Wisdom[1] [10.21]: "Wisdom opened the mouths of the dumb and gave speech to the tongues of babes.") Jesus, as so often elsewhere, in denouncing religious corruption, appeals to the great Wisdom literature of his own people, the people he deeply loved. Mark and Luke both allude to the resolve of the priests and scribes to find means of destroying Jesus, whom the masses were following in large numbers. Mark mentions that when evening came, Jesus went out of the city to lodge at Bethany. Matthew says much the same.

[1]The Wisdom of Solomon is one of the books of the Bible as known to Jesus and his contemporaries. For technical reasons it is either omitted from Protestant Bibles or relegated to the Apocrypha.

We are to understand that he went early in the morning to the Temple to teach but when evening came he left the city to lodge elsewhere.

119   Challenging the Authority of Jesus
MATTHEW 21.23-27   MARK 11.27-33   LUKE 20.1-8

When Jesus arrives at the Temple and begins teaching, the chief priests and others take the opportunity to ask him by what authority he did the things that were winning him such acclaim among the people. He parries the question by asking them what they thought of John the Baptist—has his authority been from God or from men? The priests were afraid to answer. If they said it had been from men, the masses would give trouble, for they all held that John had been a great prophet. If they said it had been from God, Jesus would have said, ''Then why didn't you believe in him?'' So they said they did not know, so declining to answer Jesus's question. Jesus responded by telling them that he also would decline to answer their question.

Never is there any point in arguing whether a person's spiritual power is or is not attuned to the divine source. For if this is not abundantly plain to the observer, nothing can possibly persuade him. If you see a person healed before your eyes and then go on to ask what right the healer has to heal, what could conceivably convince you? You do not wish to be convinced; you want very much, on the contrary, to hide from the testimony of your own eyes. If you are open to spiritual realities, then of course you will perceive God at work; if you are not, you will do all in your power to keep the blinkers over your eyes. Prejudice is a mighty force for evil of all kinds.

120   Parables that Offend the Priests
MATTHEW 21.28, 22.14   MARK 12.1-12   LUKE 20.9-19

Matthew, Mark, and Luke recount the parable of the vineyard, and Matthew adds two other similar stories. Central to the parable of the vineyard is the theme that the owner of the vineyard leased it to vinedressers. He sent one representative after another to collect the fruits, but the unworthy vinedressers abused and insulted each in turn. At length the owner sent his own son in hope that they would surely respect *him*. Instead, they killed him, thinking to grab the whole estate for themselves. The priests, correctly interpreting the parable as against themselves, would like to have laid hold of Jesus there and then, but hesitated, fearing the reaction of the people. So they decided to resort to a plot to try to catch Jesus out. They would devise specific questions with this in mind.

121 *Jesus Deals with Three Questions*

MATTHEW 22.15-40   MARK 12.13-34   LUKE 20.20-40

With the help of the Pharisees and others, the priests devised the following questions to trap Jesus. They send spies to ask him the questions so that he might the more easily be caught unawares.

The questioners begin with flattery, remarking that Jesus is known to be straight, incorruptible, fearing no man. Does he consider it right to pay tribute to Caesar? Jesus, seeing through their hypocrisy, tells them to bring him a coin. When it is handed to him he asks whose likeness is on the coin. Caesar's, of course. Then, says Jesus, give Caesar his own, and give to God what belongs to God.

On the same day, the Sadducees come with a very different question, one about the resurrection. The Pharisees accepted the resurrection. It was a belief that developed late in the history of ideas in Israel and had found acceptance only in some groups, notably the Pharisees. The Sadducees were disinclined to accept any of the newer imports among religious ideas and certainly repudiated the notion of resurrection. They were accustomed, therefore, to ask searching questions about the resurrection concept. They pose to Jesus an extreme, not to say absurd, case. When a man dies without issue, then according to the Torah his brother is to take the woman and raise offspring for his brother. (Loopholes against this had been found and it may be that in the time of Jesus the law was rarely observed with strictness; nevertheless it was still the law.) Suppose further that this brother also dies, his brother has to do the same, and so on till seven brothers have all married the same woman. At the resurrection, then, whose wife will she be? Jesus replies in effect that in the spiritual realm such questions do not arise. In the sight of God they are transcended, because God is interested in that which is living, not that which is dead. So telling was the answer that even some of the scribes themselves felicitated Jesus upon it.

Finally (according to Mark and Matthew), Jesus is asked which is the greatest commandment in the Torah. That is a tricky question, since not only are there hundreds besides the ten we all know about; even among these ten, which is to be accounted the greatest? Jesus answers by referring to the Torah itself (Deuteronomy 6.4-5 and Leviticus 19.18): love of God and neighbor. The scribe who put the question is impressed and remarks that of course this is far more important than any ritual sacrifice or other observance. Jesus, perceiving the scribe's perspicacity, observes that he is "not far from the kingdom of God."

122 *An Unanswerable Question*
MATTHEW 22.41-46   MARK 12.35-37   LUKE 20.41-44

Jesus now seeks to turn the tables on his questioners by asking them a sort of trick question. Accepting the view that David was the author of the Book of Psalms (a traditional view that is now rejected by scholars), he quotes Psalm 110.1, in which it would seem that David is referring to the Messiah and calling him "Lord." Would one call one's son "Lord"? The question seems trivial; but Jesus is trying to show that the Kingdom of God is not to be equated with the nationalist dreams of Israel. He is trying to wean his hearers from their materialistic understanding of the Kingdom that the Messiah is to usher in.

123 *The Denunciation of the Scribes and the Pharisees*

MATTHEW 23   MARK 12.38-40   LUKE 20.45-47

Jesus now denounces the recognized leaders of Israel, the Establishment, as we might say. He says they manufacture legalistic problems but take care that they are personally unaffected by any of the problems they create. They make a great show of their religion with their special dress and their grand salutations. They love to attend dinners. They will do anything to make a convert and when they do they turn him into a monster like themselves. What a fuss they make about appearances, while inside they are voracious, devouring poor widows! What a fuss they make over trivia, fastidiously straining out a gnat while swallowing a camel! As the invective reaches its climax, Jesus calls them serpents, vipers, and tells them there is no way they could escape hell.

The indictment is against all institutional religion. Sooner or later, no matter what form such religion takes, it results in the very abuses that Jesus attributes, no doubt with good reason, to the official representatives of religion in his own time and milieu. None can get off the hook.

Kierkegaard, one of the greatest religious geniuses and one of the most profoundly Christian thinkers of all time, comments on this passage in his inimitably satirical way. Jesus, in saying, "Beware of them that walk in long robes," is not criticizing sartorial custom. There is nothing wrong with long robes any more than with short ones. "If professional attire for priests had been short," he says, "Christ would have said, 'Beware of them that walk in short clothes.'" Indeed, if by convention priests had been nudists, he would have said, "Beware of them that are without clothes." The indictment holds irrespective of the form the hypocrisy takes. People who happen to dislike ceremonial and ritual often talk as though only ritualists and ceremonialists could be hypocrites; but of course one can be a hypocrite in any religion, Hindu or

Muslim, Jewish or Christian. True religion is not like any of its external forms, appearances, or observances.

Matthew concludes with the lamentation over Jerusalem that Luke has recorded elsewhere. (See Section 94.)

124   *The Poor Widow's Offering*

MARK 12.41-44   LUKE 21.1-4

Jesus illustrates his denunciation of the scribes and the Pharisees by his allusion to the widow's offering. Around a part of the Temple stood a row of boxes with openings for the receipt of offerings of money. Jesus notices the rich putting in their gifts and then a poor widow putting in two little coins. She put in more than anyone, he notes, because they were all she had, while the rich were putting in only something they had left over. The official religion-mongers, however, behave even worse, for they give only for show. In reality they are taking away from the treasury, not contributing to it. The poor widow, by contrast, is giving her all.

125   *Gentiles Seek Jesus*

JOHN 12.20-36

Among those who had come up to Jerusalem for the feast were some Greeks, presumably Greek adherents of Judaism, possibly from Decapolis. They speak to Philip (Philip is a Greek name), telling him that they wanted to see Jesus. Philip speaks to Andrew, his friend, and together they relay the request to Jesus. The Evangelist does not even tell us whether Jesus eventually saw the Greeks or not. His concern seems only to provide a cue for a great spiritual discourse by the Master.

A grain of wheat, if it does not die, remains but a grain of wheat. If, however, it falls on the ground and dies, it yields a rich harvest. That Jesus should use this imagery in the context of the Gentiles seeking Jesus is significant.

The notion of decay and rebirth was of course very familiar to the Greeks. Jesus is saying that although the wisdom he has offered to his own people has been received up to a point, it will soon seem to be forgotten. He will die and it will seem as though that is the end of him and his work. Spiritual energy, however, never dies. By laying down his life, letting go of it and finishing his work, the grain of wheat he will be planting will germinate and become a vast wheat field.

He goes on to make clear that he is talking not only of his own forthcoming death and the emergence of the Christian Way that is to arise thereafter, but also of a general principle of the spiritual realm. He who loves his life (*psychē*), he says, will lose it; he who cares not for his life will preserve it for eternal life (*zōē*). By hoarding one's life and what belongs to it as if it were a box of gold coins, one suffocates the life one cherishes; by pouring it out on others one finds life pouring back so that one is enriched a hundredfold.

Jesus then prays that "God be glorified," that is, that the divine nature be revealed, the nature of God's self-emptying love. This is a prediction of its special revelation through the terrible agony and death Jesus is about to suffer. The Evangelist tells us that then "a voice from heaven" is heard. Jesus now announces that "the Prince of this world" [Satan] will be expelled and makes the final declaration, "And when I am lifted up from the earth I shall draw all men to myself." He urges the disciples to walk in the light while they have the light to walk in, *so that they may become the sons of the Light*. He is now talking more openly than ever of the way things are in the spiritual realm. Having so spoken, "he left them and kept himself hidden."

126   *Why Jesus is Rejected*

JOHN 12.37-50

The Evangelist apparently feels constrained to provide an explanation for the fact that Jesus, despite all the wonders he has done and the popular acclaim that has attended his teaching, has been rejected by his own people. To all outward appearance he is already a failure.

Why? John suggests that the light Jesus has brought is so strong that it has blinded people. He connects the idea with prophecies in the Book of Isaiah; for instance, the notion that God actually so blinds the inner eye with the brightness of his light that people are left in darkness (Isaiah 6.9-10). Nevertheless, God has a long-term plan.

While those who are so near the light and have so much of it remain blind (see John 9.40-41), those who have less light will better appreciate Jesus. That is what it means to say that a prophet is not without honor save in his own country. Familiarity breeds contempt, not least familiarity with God. The people to whom Jesus came had a great religious tradition, a deep understanding of divine things. They had walked so close to God that they could not see his glory except through narrow slits.

That is true not only of Jesus's own people, the Jews; it is true of all who are so tied to particular forms of thought and molds of practice that they cannot grow. They are so close to the forest that they cannot see it for the trees.

The Evangelist is enunciating in his own way the truth in the old story of the hare and the tortoise. Those who are spiritually far behind and slow in their movements can often catch up with and overtake the fleet of foot who do not work so hard. It is the same principle that underlies a once-famous commercial in today's market place: ''We are only Number 2; we try harder.''

Worse even than the blind are those (some of them in high places) who see the glory of God in Jesus but are afraid to admit it because they fear being expelled from the synagogue. Again they are concerned more for appearance and the approval of men than for spiritual realities. So it is and so it has always been in the Christian Church as elsewhere. Many have preferred to hide the genuine spiritual knowledge that they possess rather than risk disapproval by others less enlightened than they.

127 Predicting the Fall of the Temple and the End of the Age

MATTHEW 24, 25   MARK 13   LUKE 21.5-38

When Jesus was still in the temple area or just leaving it, someone alluded to the grandeur of the edifice. Jesus predicted its total destruction. According to contemporary testimony from various sources, the Jerusalem Temple was indeed a grand place. Tacitus alludes to it as a "temple of immense wealth." According to Josephus, some of the stones were enormous, as much as twenty-five cubits (about 37 feet) in length. The reconstruction that had begun before the birth of Jesus (probably in the spring of 19 B.C.) was still going on during his lifetime. In A.D. 70 the Romans destroyed the Temple with their siege engines, under orders from Caesar to raze the entire city and temple to the ground. Josephus says that so complete was the destruction that nobody visiting the place thereafter would have found any reason to suppose it had ever been inhabited. So Jesus's prediction was fulfilled about forty years after his death.

Jesus also predicted the end of the age, but in doing so he issued warnings against false prophets and others who would come announcing it. Before the end, he predicted, wars and other troubles would have to be faced. Eventually, however, the end would come, attended by eclipses, earthquakes, and other cosmic phenomena. There will be terrible iniquity before the end, so much so that many will waver, but those who persevere shall be saved. He sums up his warnings and predictions and promises in one word, "Watch!" He illustrates his theme with stories and issues warnings of judgment. Things that are amiss shall be put right. The wicked shall suffer and the righteous shall be rewarded.

Judgment is indeed an ongoing moral process. What we sow we reap and the harvest we reap will be gathered in as we go along. According to the karmic principle, we reap the results of our deeds and even our inmost thoughts as we go on our pilgrimage through this and many other lives. That the age or aeon in which we live will come to an end eventually, however many billions of years the process may take, is a familiar theme in the Ancient Wisdom. One age succeeds another and each new age brings about a new kind of being. The whole process is permeated with judgment, which is the moral principle at the heart of all things. But those who learn the wisdom Jesus offers and who rely on him for their salvation have an enormous advantage. He enables them to escape the pitfalls that lead to destruction. In him, therefore, they may put their whole trust.

128 *Judas Plots to Betray Jesus*
MATTHEW 26.1-5, 14-16   MARK 14.1-2, 10-11
LUKE 22.1-6

The Passover was approaching. Jerusalem would be thronged with pilgrims coming up to Jerusalem for the feast, so the chief priests and others would have to proceed with caution. Jesus could not be taken and arrested openly. He would have to be taken by surprise. Judas facilitates the arrest. Consulting with the chief priests, he makes a deal with them. For an agreed sum of money he will deliver Jesus to them, away from the crowds of his supporters and admirers. The price was thirty pieces of silver.

129 *Preparation for the Passover*
MATTHEW 26.17-19   MARK 14.12-16   LUKE 22.7-13

Peter and John ask Jesus where he wants them to prepare the Passover. He tells them to go into the city where they will meet a man carrying a pitcher of water. They are to follow him into the house he will enter and tell him that the Master is asking the location of the dining room in which he can go with his disciples. The man will then show them an upper room with couches for reclining according to custom. The disciples set off and find everything as Jesus has predicted.

Once again we have Jesus exhibiting parapsychological powers. He knows the whole scenario around him, whom to ask, and what the reaction will be. He is reading the thoughts of all around him as if they were a book.

130 *The Last Supper*

MATTHEW 26.20-36 MARK 14.17-26
LUKE 22.14-30 JOHN 13.1-30

In the evening, Jesus is seated for the meal with his twelve disciples. A dispute arises among the disciples about precedence: which of them is the greater? Jesus, rising from supper, takes a towel and a basin of water and begins to wash the feet of the disciples and wipe them with the towel, by way of illustrating the principle that in the spiritual realm it is the superior who serves and ministers to the inferior, not the other way round as it is in the world. If he, their Master, so serves them, they ought to serve one another.

Then as they are all at table again, he announces that one of them is to betray him. The disciples express their grief at this announcement and ask who it is. Jesus identifies the traitor as the one to whom he will give a sop, the one who will dip his hand in the dish with him. It is Judas. We are to understand that Judas then takes the opportunity of leaving and steals out into the night.

In the course of the meal Jesus takes bread, making the customary *baruch* or blessing over it and saying, "This is my body, which is given for you." He then takes a cup of wine saying, "This cup is the new testament (*diathēkē*) in my blood, which is poured out for you." (Matthew says "for many".) He adds that this is the last time he will drink wine until he will "drink the new wine in the kingdom of God." The disciples eat the bread and drink of the cup, and after the singing of psalms they all go out to the Mount of Olives.

The mystical significance with which Jesus invested the eating of the bread and the drinking of the wine provided the Church with the basis for the central act of Christian worship, the Eucharist or Mass. Despite the bitter ecclesiastical controversies concerning it, this sacramental act has remained the central focus of all Christian liturgy. Jesus, building upon a customary ceremonial in his Jewish heritage, invested the symbolic act with immense spiritual significance. In Christian usage the Eucharist has acquired a threefold role: it is a memorial, a thanksgiving, and a mystical communion with the Lord and with all who are spiritually tied to him, whether on this side of the veil of death or on the other. Nowhere in the traditional practice of the Christian Way is its inner, mystical character so vividly symbolized as in the Mass or Eucharist, which Christians see as having its warrant in these words and actions of Jesus during his last meal with the disciples.

131 *Farewell Admonitions and Promises*

MATTHEW 26.31-35   MARK 14.27-31
LUKE 22.31-38   JOHN 13.31-16.33

Before his arrest, Jesus utters certain warnings and gives certain assurances to the disciples. He warns them that he is going away and that they cannot go with him. After he has gone they must love one another as he has loved them. That is how people would know that they are truly his disciples. He predicts moreover, that that very night they would all lose faith in him. Peter protests that even if all the others lose faith in the Master, he never would. To this Jesus replies that before the cock should crow in the very early morning, Peter would have disowned Jesus three times. As we shall see, that is precisely what happened.

Luke reports yet another warning Jesus gave the disciples in anticipation of his forthcoming arrest. Reminding them that when he first sent them out on their own (see

Section 61) he instructed them not to carry wallets or purses or shoes, he asks first whether they had lacked anything. They agreed that they had lacked nothing. Now, however, he tells them that the instructions are to be changed. Up to now they could always count on the hospitality of well-wishers. Despite opposition in high places there were always those who readily recognized them as bearers of the Good News of salvation. Now the prospect has changed. He is to be classed with criminals and his followers will share in the ignominy. In the future his disciples will need to fend for themselves in every way, for they must expect persecution and all sorts of trials. That proves to be indeed the case, as we learn from the Book of Acts and elsewhere. John provides an account of a long discourse by Jesus at this stage, in which Jesus promises to send the Holy Spirit to strengthen his disciples after he has left them. They will not be alone. He uses the beautiful figure of the vine and its branches to designate the mystical relation that is to exist between him and those who are mystically united to him. He warns them once more of the persecutions and sufferings they must expect but assures them that eventually their sorrow shall be turned into joy.

Finally, in a most moving passage in which Jesus strikingly alludes to the esoteric character of his teaching, he tells them that although up to now he has spoken to them in parables and figures of speech, soon will be revealed to them the secret knowledge of God. The disciples say: "Now you are speaking plainly and not using metaphors! Now we see that you know everything, and do not have to wait for questions to be put into words; because of this we believe that you came from God." Jesus, however, moderates their excitement, telling them yet again that they are about to be scattered. He is uttering these warnings "so that you may find peace in me." He concludes with the magnificent words:

In the world you will have trouble,
but be brave:
I have conquered the World.

He has conquered the world, not in the manner of a great emperor of military warrior; he has conquered it by spiritual power. Even as the hour of shame and defeat approaches fast he knows he is victorious. He knows he is one with the divine Being whence he came and whither he is returning.

132 Final Mystical Prayer for Those United with Him

JOHN 17

Jesus now "raises his eyes to heaven" and prays. His prayer, which sums up and crowns all his teachings, revealing at the same time its esoteric character, is in three parts.

First he prays for himself; second for his immediate disciples; third for all people in all ages. He asks to be glorified so that through the spiritual power over all humankind that has been given him, he may give eternal life to all who have been entrusted to him. He acknowledges that eternal life consists in knowing God. He explicitly declares that he is not praying for the world at large, he is praying for those who have been called out of the world and who "belong to you." Yet he is not asking that the faithful be removed from the world; he is asking, rather, that they be protected in the world, that is, "protected from the evil one." Finally, he prays "not only for these" but for all who will believe in him. "May they all be one. Father, may they all be one in us." He is speaking of the mystical union of the spirit. He speaks over and over again of knowing and knowledge, the knowledge that comes through love. This prayer, ablaze with the realities of the spiritual realm, is an overwhelmingly beautiful conclusion to Jesus's farewell address as well as an awesome prologue to the tragedy that is about to unfold.

133 *Gethsemane*

MATTHEW 26.36-46   MARK 14.32-42
LUKE 22.39-46   JOHN 18.1

The Garden of Gethsemane today is one of the loveliest
of the ancient holy places in Jerusalem. Unlike many of
the other areas of pilgrimage, it has not been spoiled by
commercialization. The very old and very large olive
trees give one a sense of genuine continuity with the
past, that one is walking very close to the steps of Jesus
and his disciples on the terrible night of his betrayal and
arrest. An atmosphere of calm pervades the place even
more than the holy sadness that is inevitably associated
with it. The name Gethsemane represents a Hebrew
phrase designating an oil-press used for making olive oil.
The area, at the foot of the Mount of Olives, so called
from the abundant olive trees on its slopes, would be as
natural a place for such an installation as would be a sugar
house in a maple grove. Eusebius (A.D. *c.*260 - *c.*340)
identifies it as the place where Jesus prayed before his
betrayal and arrest. It was already by that time a hallowed
place of Christian pilgrimage.

Jesus, having bidden the rest of the disciples to sit
apart, takes with him Peter, James, and John. To them he
confides his intense grief at the hostility with which his
teaching has been received. The hatred he has evoked
astonishes him. The sorrow he feels is squeezing the life
out of him (*perilypos estin hē psychē mou heōs thanatou*).
Moving apart to pray, he asks that if there be any way out
of the agony and death facing him, it may be granted to
him. He has enjoined the disciples to watch while he
prays; but when he returns he finds them asleep. "Could
you not keep watch for one hour?" he asks. He urges
them to keep vigilant, for otherwise they will weaken in
their resolve. They will need all the watchfulness they
can muster. Again he goes away to pray and again the
disciples have fallen asleep when he returns. After this,
he goes away a third time and when he finds them again
asleep, he tells them with a note of sad bitterness that now

they might as well go on sleeping, for the hour of his betrayal is at hand. John alone among the Evangelists reports nothing of these incidents, mentioning only that Jesus went over the brook Kidron "where there was a garden" with his disciples. Then he goes on to record the circumstances of the betrayal much as do the Synoptists. All the Synoptists, however, tell of the prayer and agony in Gethsemane just before the arrest.

134 The Betrayal and Arrest

MATTHEW 26.47-56
MARK 14.43-52
LUKE 22.47-53 JOHN 18.2-11

Even as Jesus is speaking, Judas appears with a crowd including armed men sent by the chief priests and elders of the Temple, bearing torches and lanterns. Judas greets Jesus with a kiss of friendship, for that has been the pre-arranged sign by which he has promised the authorities to identify his Master. Jesus, who knows of course what is in the mind and heart of Judas, remarks on the treachery in the greeting. One of the disciples (John reports that it was Peter, but the Synoptists all discreetly preserve anonymity) impulsively strikes the high priest's slave with a sword, wounding him in the ear. Jesus rebukes him with the words, "Do you think I cannot appeal to my Father who would promptly send me twelve legions of angels to my defense?" Ever in the mind of Jesus is the reality of the spiritual realm, invisible to the majority of men and women, in which the greater warfare is constantly being waged.

Only Luke tells us that high priests, officers of the Levite guard and leading Sanhedrists, were actually present. If they were it would be more specifically to them that Jesus would address the reproachful observation, "Am I a brigand that you had to set out to capture me with swords and clubs? I sat teaching in the Temple day after day and you never laid hands on me." Luke alone adds the terrible words that show how deeply Jesus was entrenched in the wisdom of the ancient gnosis in which the battleground in the spiritual realm is symbolized as a war between light and darkness. "This is your hour," he says; "this is the reign of darkness." The dark forces of the spiritual world are now ranged against him. Satan's legions are organized for war.

The disciples, terrified at the arrest of their Master, flee from the scene. Here Mark inserts a singular story about a young man, apparently a disciple of Jesus but not one of the twelve, who has presumably been awakened by the hullaboo, for he is dressed only in a linen cloth (no doubt his bed sheet), and has come to see what is happening. When someone grabs him, as perhaps they might have grabbed some of the others had they not fled, he manages to escape, leaving them with the sheet while he sprints away naked. The story is more significant than some commentators have suggested, for at least it shows why the other disciples had felt compelled to flee. Since Jesus was on the black list, association with him was obviously dangerous.

135 *The Ecclesiastical Proceedings*

MATTHEW 26.57 - 27.10   MARK 14.53-72
LUKE 22.54-71   JOHN 18.12-27

Great technical difficulties attend the description of the ecclesiastical proceedings as recounted by the four Evangelists. The accounts raise many questions and present many puzzles about the legal proceedings. A formal trial in the middle of the night, to which Mark's account points, is for several reasons extremely unlikely, to say the least. Yet that is only one of many difficulties. We really do not know much about the rules of the Sanhedrin, although it seems that they required a heretical teacher in Jerusalem to be questioned by lower courts before being taken before the Great Sanhedrin. Despite the historical difficulties, however, we can venture a fairly intelligible account of what may have happened.

John says that Jesus was *first* taken before Annas, the father-in-law of Caiaphas, the high priest that year. Annas was a retired high priest himself; he had held the office from A.D. 6 to 15, when he had been deposed by Valerius Gratus. His five sons had held the office at various intervals. So he would command much influence in the Jewish Establishment. Such a dignitary would no doubt seem eminently qualified to sit as a sort of court of inquiry and so fulfill the spirit, if not the letter, of the requirement of appearance before a lower court in the first instance.

Be that as it may, John mentions that Jesus was bound, presumably his hands tied behind his back, when taken before Annas, who asked him about his disciples and his teaching. Jesus gives very able answers, telling Annas that since all his teaching had been conducted openly and often in the synagogues and in the presence of many Jews of all walks of life, there was no need to rely on his own testimony; the court could ask any of the numerous individuals who had often heard him teach. A guard interpreted this as insolence and cuffed Jesus. But Annas probably saw that Jesus was sincere and perhaps saw, moreover, that the simplest solution to the whole problem as he understood it would be to get Jesus executed. It would be very easy for Annas to convey this in a note or message to Caiaphas before whom Jesus eventually would be taken. It seems that Annas did not detain him very long.

The place where these proceedings occurred is not clear, but it may have been in the courtyard of the house of Caiaphas. At any rate, we may suppose that it was somewhere in the vicinity that Peter was standing, lingering to see what was happening, when a maid on duty at the door thought she recognized him as a disciple of the accused. She asked him pointedly and he replied categorically that he was not. As Peter stands warming himself at the outdoor fire, for it would be a chilly spring night, somebody else recognized him and likewise challenged him, receiving the same categorical denial. According to Matthew, Peter's Galilean accent had given him away. Finally, one of the high priest's servants who had been in the Garden of Gethsemane recognized him and asked the same question, receiving also the same denial. Immediately the cock crew as Jesus had predicted. Luke adds that at this point Jesus, who was either within earshot or knew by clairvoyance of the scene, turned around "and looked upon Peter." Whether we are to suppose that he was within sight of Peter at the time, which seems unlikely, or that Luke is telling us that Peter inwardly saw the Master's eyes turning upon him in reproach, the effect on Peter was devastating. He went out sobbing bitterly, for as he went the loving eyes of Jesus pierced his inmost soul.

Although the sequence of events is obscure, we may suppose that Jesus spent the rest of the night in custody in the house or palace of the high priest and that early in the morning the Sanhedrin convened, either there or in the Council Hall (*bouleutērion*) on the west side of the Temple precincts not far from the high-priest's palace. If this court were to be able to find any grounds for handing Jesus over to the Roman governor for execution, it would have to establish some offense against the political order showing him to be dangerous to the sovereignty of the Emperor. The Romans would not be interested in Jewish theological questions. It was necessary, too, to obtain witnesses. Witnesses of sorts had been apparently cajoled or bribed into giving testimony; but it seems they were not much good as witnesses for the prosecution. The best they were able to allege was that Jesus had said something about destroying the Temple and rebuilding it in three days. This could easily be interpreted as, "I am going to destroy the Temple," which would be a threat to the existing order. Still, it sounded more like the ravings of a crazy fanatic than of a serious enemy of the State. When Caiaphas asks Jesus directly, "Are you the Messiah?" Jesus answers directly, "*Ani hu*" (I am), adding that he would be coming on the clouds of heaven to judge all men. At this Caiaphas rends his tunic to express formally his pretense of sorrow. Jesus, in claiming to be the Messiah, the promised King, is guilty of treason against Caesar.

He ought, therefore, to be handed over to the Roman authorities with a recommendation for execution.

We must understand the situation of these Jewish leaders. The common people distrusted them because of their subservience to the Roman authorities. These grandees in the Jewish system knew this. They knew, moreover, that they were in a precarious position, poised between their own people, on the one hand, and, on the other, the Roman authorities whom they had to please in order to keep their hereditary positions of influence and power. The uncompromising attitude of Jesus had not only angered but frightened them. He was a threat to their positions, enjoying as he did, so much popular support. Plainly, the sooner he was out of the way the better.

They take him to Pilate as early as possible that very morning. Meanwhile, we are told, Judas has second thoughts when he sees what is going to happen, what his treachery has made possible. Repenting, he comes back to the authorities with the thirty pieces of silver; but his offer is scorned. Then Judas throws the money down and goes out and hangs himself. The authorities, legalistic to the end, find that they cannot use the money for holy purposes because it is "the price of blood"; but they buy with it a piece of land for use as a cemetery for foreigners.

136   *The Trial Before Pilate*

MATTHEW 27.11-31   MARK 15.1-20
LUKE 23.1-25   JOHN 18.28 - 19.16

Arraigned before Pilate, Jesus is charged with political subversion. He has been forbidding the payment of tribute to Caesar and claiming to be King. The tribunal is held in the Herodian Palace on the west of the city, near what is today the Jaffa Gate. It is the Roman procurator's official residence in Jerusalem. Pilate, probably doubtful about a charge brought to him peremptorily so early in the morning, suggests that they deal with it themselves. To this they reply that they cannot, since they have recently been deprived of the power to execute criminals. Pilate, more and more annoyed, asks Jesus if he thinks he is the King of the Jews. The reply Jesus gives is in the form of a question that is certainly not calculated to mollify the governor. "Do you ask this of your own accord or have other people been talking to you about me?"

The irritated Pilate points out that it is the chief priests of Jesus's own people who have brought the charge. What exactly has Jesus done to rouse their anger? When Jesus tells him that his Kingdom is "not of this world," not of the existing world order, Pilate probably concludes that he has before him a man whose mind is deranged. To talk to a practical Roman administrator such as Pilate, of a kingdom beyond this world would have been almost like someone today talking science fiction to an IRS auditor.

"Then you *are* a king?" asks Pilate, no doubt with the tolerant smile that any judge might give to an obviously crazy person. When Jesus replies that he is indeed a king and has come into the world to witness to that truth, Pilate must have been absolutely certain that an insane religious fanatic had come before him. The case was of no concern to a serious court. How is he to get rid of it? He murmurs with a touch of mockery, "Truth? What is truth?" Then he jumps up and announces that he could see no case at all.

Luke tells us that at this point the accusers press their charge, arguing that Jesus has been inciting the people to rebellion all over the province. He has begun doing so in Galilee and now he is doing it here. At this Pilate inquires if the accused is a Galilean. He is? Then in that case, says Pilate, contriving to get himself off the hook, he should be tried by Herod Antipas, the tetrarch of Galilee.

Herod was in Jerusalem for the Passover and was staying at the Hasmonean Palace not far away. He had been for some time rather curious to see this Jesus about whom he had heard so much, so he was glad of the opportunity that presented itself. When he questions Jesus while the accusers renewed their charges with increasing vehemence, Jesus maintains a silence as exasperating as it is puzzling. Herod may have been ill-disposed toward Jesus in the first place. After all, Jesus had called him "that fox" (Luke 13.32). Yet there is no evidence for Herod's ill will. We are told only that Herod teases and mocks Jesus and gets his soldiers to put a grand robe on him as a joke.

At length Herod sends Jesus back to Pilate with a message to the effect that he seems to be a harmless fool. Pilate and Herod happened to be at odds with one another, perhaps because Pilate's soldiers had killed Galileans in a demonstration about the seizure of certain funds. According to Luke, the case that they both took to be a frivolous charge against a religious maniac brought them together.

The prosecution is now faced with a troublesome situation. This time they bring along a mob of slaves and anybody else they can muster to fill the courtyard of the praetorium. Pilate still can see no reason for the execution they demanded. He suggests a compromise: have Jesus whipped and then released in accordance with a custom to grant amnesty to a prisoner at the Passover season. The servile crowd, naturally seeking to please the priestly Establishment, yells that Barabbas, another prisoner, should be released rather than Jesus. Pilate, who disliked Jews, would probably see an ulterior motive on the part of the prosecution. He orders Jesus to be whipped and has the guards dress him up afterwards in a grand cloak with a crown of thorns on his head. Then, mocking the crowd as much as the prisoner, he tells them: "There you are! There is your king!" Nevertheless, with all the irrationality of crowds they yell over and over again, "Crucify! Crucify!" Pilate takes water and washes his hands to symbolize his repudiation of the whole affair. As the crowd of Jews and Gentiles yell on, however, the prosecution comes up with the argument that if Pilate were to release Jesus he would be acting against Caesar, for the prisoner has claimed to be a king and they want no king but Caesar. This is the argument that seems to have intimidated Pilate. He could not afford even the slightest hint of disloyalty to the Emperor. So the prosecution wins. Barabbas is released and Jesus sentenced to crucifixion.

Only a word need be said here about the old notion, now discredited by all reputable scholars, that the Jews as a people were responsible for the death of Jesus. On the contrary, multitudes of Jews had obviously welcomed Jesus and loved him. Many, too, hated the Establishment and eventually revolted against it. Jesus was a Jew who deeply loved his own people. When he chided or rebuked them he did so from within the Jewish family, the Jewish people, into whose fold he had been born. Who, then, may be said to be responsible for the monstrous sentence of crucifixion?

The story, however we may reconstruct it, is a paradigm of the evil that politicking, especially religious politicking, habitually achieves. Given the circumstances, the outcome could hardly have been otherwise.

Any intelligent observer anywhere in the world, knowing these circumstances, could have written the script for what happened. In the trial of Jesus we see the archetype of all the appalling injustice that is typically engendered by organizational hierarchies and institutional bureaucracies. The personal spite of his prosecutors and the callous indifference of his judges are as nothing to the cruelty of the system that made possible the implementation of the demand of the insensate mob. Mob rule ensures injustice of every kind, for it is always the vilest of men and women who are best situated and can make themselves best equipped to use crowds for evil purposes. If we must find a scapegoat for such appalling injustice we might as well make it the crowd of servile henchman—Jewish and Gentile—howling the sentence that Pilate ratified. Yet the crowd was only the outward vesture of the organizational machine, the total political situation, Jewish aristocracy and Roman administration, of which Jesus was the victim. It is such machinery that victimizes the individual; the nobler the individual the viler the victimization. Jesus, the incarnation of divine Being, is supremely individual.

137 Crucifixion

MATTHEW 27.32-56   MARK 15.21-41
LUKE 23.26-49   JOHN 19.17-37

Crucifixion was an especially cruel punishment, not inflicted on Roman citizens but only on slaves and foreigners guilty of heinous crimes such as murder, robbery, and treason. The cross was usually either T-shaped or dagger-shaped. Since in the case of Jesus the description of his offense was inscribed above his head, according to Matthew 27.37, the dagger-shaped cross was probably used, as traditionally represented in Christian art. The upright beam was usually placed in the ground; the prisoner carried only the crossbeam to the place of execution. He was then laid on the ground and attached to the crossbeam, then lifted with the crossbeam and fastened to the upright. The nails would go into the wrists, not the hands as generally depicted in art, and it is noteworthy in passing that the Holy Shroud of Turin shows the imprint of the nails in that way, not on the hands. Victims were generally crucified naked and it is likely that the custom would be followed in the case of Jesus. The victim's clothing was customarily given to the soldiers as a sort of bonus. Around the victim's neck was generally hung a brief description of his crime—murderer, thief, and the like. By a kind of macabre joke, Pilate had officially dubbed him "King of the Jews," and this was inscribed in three languages, Hebrew (or Aramaic), Greek, and Latin, so that all might understand it. The victim might be left to die of hunger, thirst, and exposure. We are led to understand that the soldiers were surprised that Jesus died so quickly. Modern medical opinion seems inclined to the view that death would have occurred in his case from a kind of asphyxiation, deprivation of oxygen to the brain. The punishment of crucifixion was an import from the Orient introduced to the West from Iran. One of the most barbarously cruel punishments ever devised, it was abolished in the West by Constantine, the first Christian emperor, in the fourth century.

Christian piety traditionally venerates "the seven last words" of Jesus. While there is no reason to suppose that they constitute all he said in his last hours, there are various reasons supporting their authenticity.

One is of peculiar interest to us here. Along with Jesus were crucified also two notorious thieves, one of whom derides Jesus. But the other, perhaps sensing that he is in the presence of great holiness, says, "Jesus, remember me when you come into your kingdom." In reply Jesus promises, "Today you will be with me in paradise." "Paradise" (Hebrew, *pardēs*; Greek, *paradeisos*) is a loan-word from Old Persian where it was used to designate a walled garden such as one would expect in a palace or the like. The notion was variously interpreted, however, and might also represent an intermediate state between the present life and one's eventual destiny, whatever that might be. If we take literally this promise of Jesus to the "good thief," it must surely require to be understood in some such way, since according to the Gospels Jesus "rose from the dead" on "the third day" and it was many days more before he "ascended into heaven." That what Jesus intended was the state in the subtle or astral body after death seems plausible.

Another of these utterances of Jesus on the cross is of profound signficance: *Eli, Eli lama sabachthani?*-"My God, my God, why hast thou forsaken me?" In the Qumran psalms the "Teacher of Righteousness" often says "Thou hast not forsaken me." Yet Jesus in his agony affirms the opposite. He who is fully divine yet also fully human must experience the depth of human spiritual anguish, the sense of the absence of God. God is sometimes better known through his absence than through his presence, as water is better appreciated by a man dying of thirst in the desert than by one sitting amid living springs. To the physical agonies Jesus suffers and the mental anguish he endures is added the final spiritual deprivation, the sense of desertion by God.

At three o'clock in the afternoon by our modern way of reckoning, the Temple trumpets would sound, announcing the hour of prayer, when the faithful would be saying the beautiful prayer: "In thy hands are the souls of all the living and the dead....Into thy hands I commend my spirit. Thou hast redeemed me, O Lord, thou God of truth....In the name of the Lord, the God of Israel: may Michael be at my right hand, Gabriel at my left hand, before me Uriel, behind me Raphael, and above my head the presence of God." Jesus probably uses a shortened form of it such as he would have learned in childhood from his Mother, Mary, who with some of the other women stands near the cross weeping. Custom dictated that the words should be uttered in a loud voice. Jesus, using the simpler form, may have said: "Abba, into thy hands I commit my spirit." So saying, he yields up his spirit. When the soldiers come to check the bodies of the victims and break their bones to hasten their end, they find Jesus is already dead.

138 *The Burial*

MATTHEW 27.57-66   MARK 15.42-47
LUKE 23.50-56   JOHN 19.38-42

All the Gospels relate that a certain rich man, Joseph of Arimathaea, a member of the Sanhedrin, asked Pilate as a favor, to give him the body of Jesus. Normally, the bodies of crucified persons were left to hang on the cross. The town to which this Joseph belonged was Ramah (Arimathaea is the Greek form of the name) in the hill country of Ephraim, located by modern scholars at what is now Rentis, a village on the west edge of the Ephraim hills on the road leading through the valley from the coastal plain to Shiloh. It as an ancient town in which a thousand years earlier Samuel had been buried.

According to John, Joseph was secretly a disciple of Jesus. Accompanied by Nicodemus, also apparently a secret disciple, he removed the body. There was very little time, for the Sabbath would begin that evening, a few hours after the death of Jesus. They brought an enormous quantity of spices for the burial, a hundred pounds, John says. With the pound equal to about eleven ounces in our reckoning, that would be something like seventy pounds. The spices, to be used in a speedy form of embalming (since there would be no time for anything more elaborate), consisted of a mixture of myrrh and aloes. Myrrh was produced from the gum resin of a small tree, *commiphora myrrha*. The aromatic gum was obtained by piercing the bark. When the gum is exposed to the air it hardens and turns red. Aloes, much used in biblical times as a perfume for a variety of purposes including burial, was an aromatic oil obtained from a tree indigenous to India. They took the body and wrapped it up in the spices, using bandages according to custom and a linen shroud.

Luke tells us that after the burial the women return and prepare spices and ointments for use *after* the Sabbath. Mark also, in his account of what happened after the Sabbath, indicates that they brought spices to the tomb. This is not entirely inconsistent with John's account, for since love knows no bounds the women might well have wished to perform their act of devotion in a less hurried way as soon as opportunity arose after the Sabbath.

Jesus had been crucified at a place call Golgotha, the exact location of which cannot be determined with absolute certainty, although it was beyond, and probably not far beyond, the city walls. The traditional site is marked by the Church of the Holy Sepulchre. At any rate, near the spot was an orchard. Since Joseph's own tomb was there, it may have been his property. Another tomb, so far never used, was available, and that was where they took Jesus and laid him. It was probably a grave hewn out of the hillside rock. It was customary to secure such a grave with a heavy stone to make it safe against wild animals and other possible intruders. No doubt such a stone, probably a round one and set in a groove, was used in the case of Jesus. The incident that Matthew adds, which is absent from the accounts of all the other Evangelists, presents some difficulties. It is not, however, fundamentally important and we may ignore it.

The accounts of the use of the spices, on the other hand, might be of great significance in connection with the famous relic that has been preserved at Turin for many centuries and venerated as the shroud or burial cloth of Jesus, since chemicals in them (if the shroud be authentic) might have been a factor in the preservation of the image on the cloth. This image consists of a positive imprint of a human body on the front and back. It includes the mark of nails, one in each wrist, which accords with what is now known to have been the practice and is contrary to traditional representations, which show the nails in the hands.

Although the history of this remarkable relic cannot be traced with certainty beyond the fourteenth century, and we are all well aware of the widespread fabrication of relics as "pious frauds," the shroud is a very special case. It has been examined in recent years with immense care and with the scientific tools and methods available today and, although the results so far have been inconclusive, nothing has emerged to disprove the relic's authenticity. Many eminent scientists an medical authorities in Italy and throughout the world, some of whom have no prior disposition toward belief in such a story, have become increasingly impressed by the evidence and inclined to regard the relic as quite possibly authentic. One hindrance to progress in the investigation so far has been the fact that a Carbon 14 test that could determine within a half century or so the date of the material would have entailed the destruction of a large area, probably several square feet. The custodians of the relic have been naturally unwilling to permit that part of the scientific examination. This difficulty, however, may be overcome. More will be said of this relic in Appendix I.

X

THE VESTURE OF LIGHT

139 *Jesus in Risen Glory Nearby His Grave*

MATTHEW 28.1-15   MARK 16.1-11
LUKE 24.1-12   JOHN 20.1-18

All four Evangelists, despite some slight discrepancies in their respective accounts, attest that the mourning women rose while it was still dark on the day after the Sabbath, and that they find the tomb empty. All speak of an angel (Matthew says his appearance was as lightning and his vesture white as snow) or angels (Luke alludes to their "dazzling apparel") at or near the burial place. The purpose of the women's visit was to attend to the funeral rites more adequately than would have been possible in the few hours before the Sabbath. They find, however, that the stone has been rolled away and the body of Jesus is gone. They rush back to Peter and John to tell them what they have seen. Peter and John are incredulous, supposing that the women are emotionally upset.

John provides considerable detail. Like the other Evangelists he says that Peter and John come to the tomb to see for themselves, but he reports that they run and that

John outruns Peter, getting first to the tomb. (This is as one would expect, since he was the younger man and would be likely to be able to run faster.) John glances down and looks inside the tomb and sees the linen cloths lying there, but he does not go inside, presumably being petrified with astonishment. Peter then arrives and goes inside, where he also sees the linen cloths lying. The napkin that had been round the head of Jesus is folded up by itself, a little apart from the other bandages. Then John goes inside too and is convinced: Jesus must have risen from the dead.

The same Evangelist goes on to tell us that Mary Magdalene is standing nearby weeping. In her distress she glances again at the tomb. Inside she sees two angels, the one at the place where the head of Jesus had been, the other at the place where the feet had rested. They ask her why she is weeping, and she tells them that it is because they have taken away her master and she does not know where they have put him. She turns round and, in the half-dark, she notices someone standing. She assumes it is the gardener, since he would be the only person likely to be around at the very early hour. She hears the figure say, "Why are you sobbing? Who are you looking for?" She does not answer directly. Instead she pleads, "Sir, if you've taken him away, tell me where you have put him and I'll go and remove him." Then the figure, speaking out of the half-darkness, utters her name—"Mary!"

In a flash of recognition at his speaking her name, she turns arounds and sees it is Jesus.

"*Rabbouni!*" she exclaims delightedly, using the Aramaic expression: not merely "teacher" or "master" or "rabbi" but "*my* teacher, *my* master, *my* rabbi."

As she speaks she instinctively runs forward to embrace him, but he resists her embrace, explaining that he has not yet "ascended to the Father"; that is, he is still hovering among his friends on earth. Only when he has fully entered into the spiritual dimension whither he is bound will she and the others be able to understand and enjoy the reality of his presence. Meanwhile she cannot cling to him as she wishes, because his body is a "glorified one."

We may say it is a "body of light."

This physical body of ours, the "flesh" that the Logos took on in "becoming man," is, we now know, infinitely more complex than it looks. It is not mere physical complexity that makes it so astonishing, although that is remarkable enough (35 miles of glomerular capillaries in our two little kidneys, for example, and 12 billion nerve cells in a brain that weighs no more than a fairly fat little book, about 45 - 50 ounces). What is even more awesome is the sub-microscopic complexity of the human body, its nuclear structures, the intricacy of its psychic arrangements. The physiological involutions are mere pointers to a far more baffling psychic complexity beyond them. That we shed this body at death and continue in an alternate "astral" body is an ancient view that is becoming more and more plausible in the light of modern scientific inquiry. In the case of one so far beyond other men as was Jesus, the energy released at death might well have had far more startling consequences than those that would be generally expected. The possibility that this tremendous explosion of energy might self-destruct his "flesh-and-bones" body and roll away the stone securing the tomb is not to be ruled out, absurd as it might have seemed to the skeptical among our forefathers.

The women and Peter and John go back and tell the rest of the eleven disciples what strange things they have seen and heard. John alone tells us that Mary Magadalene actually saw and talked with the risen Jesus; but all the Evangelists record the discovery by Peter and John of the empty tomb.

140 *The Walk in Emmaus*

MARK 16.12-13   LUKE 24.13-35

This most beautiful narrative is fraught with parapsychological content and esoteric significance. Luke alone relates it in detail.

Identification of the village of Emmaus, which the text says lay about sixty stadia or furlongs (about seven miles) from Jerusalem, has puzzled many scholars, since no village corresponding to that name is known to answer that description. It could not be the modern Amwas, since that town is much too far away. It might be, however, the modern Kaloniyeh, which is about four miles; the Evangelist may have miscalculated the distance. Four miles would make the round trip an eight-mile walk, which even for those days would be a considerable distance.

Two disciples of Jesus, apparently not of the eleven, are walking to the village of Emmaus. They are disconsolate at the thought of the appalling tragedy, the cruel death of Jesus. As they walk, a man overtakes them and walks alongside. He asks what they are discussing. One of them, called Cleopas, remarks that he must surely be the only person in Jerusalem who has not heard of the terrible things that have happened.

"What things?" asks their new companion of the road.

They tell him all. The stranger then chides them: "Foolish men! How slow you are to believe the prophets! Don't they predict that the Messiah must suffer before entering into his glory?" (He is presumably alluding to Isaiah 53: the concept of the Suffering Servant.) Then he begins expounding the Scriptures to them, beginning with Moses and "going through all the prophets."

When they reach the village "he makes as if to go on," but they press him to have a meal with them and stay overnight, for he has entranced them with this exposition of the Scriptures and they want to hear more from this fascinating, learned stranger.

He eventually accepts their invitation and goes home with them. They all sit down to eat and as they do so he takes the bread in the customary fashion for blessing. As he blesses the bread, something in his demeanor must have alerted them, for suddenly they recognize that the stranger is Jesus. And in their flash of recognition he has "vanished from their sight."

Excitedly they talk to each other of the marvellous insights he has opened up to them as he has been expounding the Scriptures. Then they walk back to Jerusalem to report the episode to the eleven, who tell them that their news does not surprise them as much as might have been expected for, they say, Jesus "has risen and appeared to Simon." Then Cleopas and his companion tell in detail the story of how the stranger has made up to them on the road and how they have recognized him "in the breaking of the bread."

Why did not they recognize the risen Lord as soon as he overtook them on the road? The Evangelist says that "something prevented them." Jesus himself, in his risen power, had chosen to disguise himself from them while he was disclosing to them the esoteric meaning of the Scriptures, as he had then chosen to reveal his identity in the sacred moment of the blessing of the bread, before vanishing from them.

The story is told with haunting grace and charm. Everything happens so naturally until the dramatic moment of the blessing, when suddenly they recognize the Master. Anyone accustomed to parapsychological phenomena will not only readily understand but appreciate the extraordinary beauty of the episode. In the spiritual realm action is not hampered by the limitations of our physical bodies or the restrictions that circumscribe their movements. Cleopas and his companion were still novices in spirituality, not yet endowed with much clairvoyance. Jesus chose to teach them to understand their own prophetic tradition in the light of the Ancient Wisdom. His exegesis of the prophets was as different from the conventional exegeses as it had always been; yet not till they had seen him in sacramental action did they see the light. Only then "their eyes were opened."

The notion that the Christ walks in the stranger's guise has been widely recognized in Christian thought throughout the ages. It is beautifully expressed in the old Gaelic rune:

I saw a stranger yestereen;
I put food in the eating place,
  Drink in the drinking place,
  Music in the listening place;

And in the sacred name of the Triune
He blessed me and my house
  My cattle and my dear ones.
And the lark said in her song:
    Often, often, often,
Goes the Christ in the stranger's guise;
    Often, often, often,
Goes the Christ in the stranger's guise.

Strangers, having no rank, no profession, no social security number, no niche in society at all, can be emissaries from the spiritual world and even, as on the road to Emmaus, Jesus himself in risen glory.

141 *The Disciples in Jerusalem See the Risen Lord*

MARK 16.14   LUKE 24.36-43   JOHN 20.19-29

Between Luke's and John's account of this incident is a notable discrepancy. Both agree that Jesus suddenly appeared in the midst of them, greeting them with the customary salutation: *shalom elechem,* "Peace be with you!" Luke emphasized the initial skepticism of the disciples. Both Luke and John report that Jesus showed them the imprint of the nails in his body. While John, however, pointedly notes that it was evening and the doors were shut when Jesus suddenly appeared, Luke says that Jesus actually asked for something to eat and, on receiving a piece of broiled fish, took it and ate it "before their eyes." In the one case he walks through closed doors; in the other he eats fish.

We may suppose, if we will, that a materialization occurred such as would make Luke's account intelligible. But many prefer to take John's account as the normative one and to regard Luke's at this point as manifesting a tendency in him to clothe spiritual realities with corporeal habiliments. Whatever our choice, we should bear in mind that the connection between spirit and body is far more marvellous than we are commonly inclined to suppose. What the disciples saw and heard was no mere apparition projected by their minds, but a real presence that they encountered and with whom they joyfully conversed.

It was precisely on such repeated experiences of meet-the Risen Lord that the faith of Christians was based. We cannot too often remind ourselves that if nothing had happened after the shame and tragedy of Good Friday, then nothing even remotely resembling the rise of the Christian Way could ever conceivably have taken place. It may be an exaggeration to say, as some have suggested, that on Good Friday there was only one Christian and he was dead on a cross; but it does bring home the inescapable truth that it was these Resurrection encounters that moved the disciples to active apostleship of the new Way. The Resurrection was indisputably at the very heart of the apostolic proclamation of the Good News: "*Christos anestē*, Christ is risen!" was their habitual greeting, the essence of their teaching.

When Jesus appeared to the disciples in Jerusalem, Thomas happened to be absent. On hearing the story, he expressed his doubts. He was too overwhelmed by the gloom they had all experienced as a result of the tragic events of Good Friday to be able to share their ecstasy. "Unless I can see for myself the mark of the nails and put my fingers on the place, and put my hand in his side, I decline to believe"; that is, he would suppose that the rest of the eleven had projected an image of the Lord out of their heads in fulfillment of their own wishes.

A week after the first appearance, however, when the eleven were assembled, presumably for weekly worship, the doors of the house were closed again as before and once again Jesus suddenly appeared in their midst, saying as usual: *shalom elechem*. Then he spoke to Thomas:

"Put your finger here; look, here are my hands. Give me *your* hand; put it into my side. Don't doubt any longer! Believe!"

"My Lord and my God!" exclaimed Thomas, to which Jesus said, "You believe because you see me. Happy are those who have not seen and yet have believed."

It is not always necessary to see a spiritual presence or to hear it or touch it. There are many impediments to our doing so, arising from a variety of sources that include our general insensitivity to the spiritual realities around us. The ability to be aware of spiritual presences is infinitely more important than seeing them clairvoyantly or otherwise. Such awareness is indeed the most profound kind of clairvoyance. In the case of Jesus, who is now clearly acclaimed as God, as he was in the prologue that comprises the first section of the present study, that presence overwhelmed the disciples.

The Risen Lord commissions the disciples to go out as his ambassadors, his apostles. He breathes on them, enjoining them to receive his spirit. ("Spirit" and "breath" are linguistically connected in the biblical languages.) He tells them that they are to have the spiritual power to forgive sins and to withhold forgiveness. That is to say, they are to be the channels through which Christian forgiveness is normally to flow. It does not mean that divine Being restricts his love to an institutionally restricted channel. It does mean, however, that such is the design he proposes for the working of the Christian communities that Jesus, by divine precognition, sees emerging all over the Mediterranean lands and beyond.

142 *Some Disciples Meet the Risen Lord Again*

JOHN 21.1-24

The Evangelist John tells us that at a later time Jesus also discloses himself (*ephanerōsen heauton*) to some disciples. He mentions Peter, Thomas, Nathanael, James, John (the two "sons of Zebedee"), and two others whom he does not name. In this account Peter says to the others, "I'm going fishing."

The others reply, "We'll come with you."

Then off they all go into the boat; but all night long they catch nothing. The day dawns, which means that the best time for fishing is over. A man standing on the beach calls to them, "Have you caught anything, boys?" (The Greek *paidia* means precisely that; therefore the racy-sounding English rendering is fully justified.) When they say "no" he says, "Throw the net out to starboard and you'll find something!" They do so and the catch is so enormous that at first they cannot haul it ashore. They are about a hundred yards from the beach.

At this point John apparently nudges Peter, saying, "It's the Lord!" (Again and again John shows himself to be more clairvoyant than the other disciples.) At this Peter, who has been stripped for work, throws some sort of fisherman's blouse over himself and leaps into the water, while the others come in gradually towing the net with the fish in it. As they reach the shore they see that Jesus already has a meal in preparation, bread to go with the fish. When he tells them to bring some of the fish they have caught, Peter unfastens the net and brings in the catch which, despite its great weight, has not broken the net. Then Jesus says, "Come and eat breakfast."

The Evangelist mentions that nobody asked the stranger who he was, because they "knew it was the Lord." Perhaps, as in the Emmaus story, we are to understand that it was at the blessing of the food that they fully recognized him. We are told that Jesus "stepped forward," took the bread and the fish, and gave them to the disciples; but nowhere in this account is there any mention of his having actually partaken of the food himself. John adds that this was "the third time" that Jesus appeared to the disciples after he had "risen from the dead."

Jesus then talks very solemnly to Peter, drawing him aside and asking him, "Do you love me more than the others do?"

"Of course — you *know* I love you."

Then Jesus says, "Feed my lambs." Peter must show his love by nourishing those who are babes in the spiritual realm. Again Jesus asks the same question and this time he enjoins Peter to be a shepherd to his sheep, that is, to guide those who are advancing in spirituality. When Jesus for the third time asks the question, Peter seems annoyed at the repetition. "Lord," he says, "you know *everything* (*panta su oidas*); you *know* that I love you." Peter's own love for the Master gives him the intuitive knowledge that Jesus is well aware of his love. Then Jesus says finally, "Feed my sheep." Even those who have attained some maturity in the spiritual realm need to be nourished too.

But Jesus then speaks to Peter more earnestly still, warning him that although now he has full control of his body and can go wherever he pleases, the time will come when he will grow old and someone else will have to dress him and take him where he has no desire to go. The Evangelist sees in this a prediction of the kind of death Peter is to die. According to Origen, an early Christian Father, Peter, when he was eventually crucified in the year A.D. 64, asked to be crucified upside down since he was unworthy to be crucified in exactly the same was as the Master.

Then Peter, catching sight of John, asks, "What about *him*?"

To this Jesus gives an important answer: "If I want him to stay behind till I return, what does that matter to you? You are to follow me."

Discipleship is a personal matter. One disciple may be called to this kind of service, another to a different one. According to the text, this saying of Jesus was misunderstood in the Christian community to mean that John was not to die. Jesus, however, did not say that. He was only pointing out that the service of one disciple is not to be the concern of the others. It is a matter between the individual and his Lord. There are as many ways of service, as there are "many mansions" in the life to come.

143 *On a Mountain in Galilee*

MATTHEW 28.16-20   MARK 16.15-18

Matthew relates that the eleven disciples encountered Jesus on a mountain in Galilee where he had arranged to

meet them. They bowed down before him. Some, however, were in doubt. Presumably we are to understand
that the clairvoyance of some was keener than that of
others. It was here, according to Matthew, that Jesus gave
the final commission to the eleven: they are to go out into
the world and make disciples "of all the nations," baptizing them in the Triune Name. He promised, moreover,
that he would be with them always, even to the end of the
age.

144 *The Final Parting and Ascension*

LUKE 24.44-53

According to Luke, after the appearance of Jesus to the
eleven at Jerusalem, he "opened their minds to understand the Scriptures." The clear implication is that they
had not properly understood the Scriptures before and
that he is now teaching them a wisdom hitherto hidden
from them. He enjoins them moreover, to wait in Jerusalem till they would be "clothed with power from on
high." They are going to be given spiritual power to fulfill
their commission, but they must wait a little to receive
it.

Then he took them to the outskirts of Bethany and as
he blessed them he "withdrew from them and was carried
up to heaven." This, along with a similar reference in
Acts 1.9-11, constitutes the only allusion in the New
Testament to the notion of the ascension of Christ, which
has been a favorite subject in Christian painting, often
very crudely represented. A text in Ephesians (4.10) is
noteworthy: he "ascended far *above* the heavens, that he
might fill all things." In other words, he went beyond our
customary range of existence to another dimension of
being. Some Christian painters, in fact, have kaleido-
scoped the resurrection and ascension as though they
were one event. Examples are to be found in the works of
Fra Angelica, Verrocchio, Perugino, and others. This is
significant, since it suggests that the great change has
occurred in the tomb. The risen Lord then continues to

hover near his friends for some weeks and then withdraws himself, since it is better that he should fill the whole spiritual realm with his energy.

145 *Many Other Things*

JOHN 20.30-31; 21.25

In the concluding section of John's Gospel are two references to things *not* recorded in the text. There were many other signs that the disciples saw that are not recorded. If all the things that Jesus did could be written down, the Evangelist surmises, the whole world could not contain the books that would be needed to record them. What we have are but samples illustrative of the kind of things he did, the kind of person he was. In particular, his teaching went far beyond what is recorded. Its full import would be beyond the understanding of most of the disciples at first. Only by degrees would its significance unfold itself to them as they followed his precept to teach others.

He who teaches learns, runs the old proverb. The depth of divine wisdom the disciples must have imbibed at the feet of the Master was far beyond what can be contained in any record such as the Gospels. They could have appropriated only a surface layer at the time of hearing him. He planted the seed in their hearts and minds. Gradually it bloomed.

For spiritual truth is not learned like the alphabet or the multiplication table. Like a great tree, it must be planted deep down and lie seemingly dormant for awhile until at last it begins to send forth its shoots. What we have in the Gospels, as is here attested, is but a token of the spiritual realities to which they point. Yet in them is a pointer to the way that leads to the full appropriation of the truths we need so much to understand in the course of our long pilgrimage to everlasting joy.

CONCLUSION

In the Introduction to this book we saw that the Gospels were not conceived by their authors as strictly historical narratives such as we should expect today, and that therefore we cannot hope either to construct a clear chronological account of them or to rely on them for accurate detail. Nevertheless, we are not to conclude that we know nothing, or next to nothing, of the life and work of Jesus. On the contrary, as anyone who has read the preceding chapters with even the slightest care must see, we are able to catch not merely glimpses but a vivid impression of Jesus as he moves about, teaching and healing. What we find is startling.

He is a rabbi, but a most unusual one. He teaches in synagogues as would any other; but he also teaches on hillsides, on lake shores, from boats, and indeed wherever people gather, as they constantly do, to hear him. His hearers are unconventional too. They include women and children (unusual in his milieu), tax collectors, harlots, and lepers. True, by his time Judaism had many faces, offering many alternatives and permitting several schools of thought. His method and manner, however, seem to strike everyone as singular. The conventional rabbi interpreted the Bible, often with much ingenuity and great learning, but always at a distance from his sources, the Torah and the Prophets. Even at the best he would give his hearers the impression that an intelligent and interested lay audience today would have in listening to an academic lecture by a professor of law. Jesus, although he was nothing if not learned in the law, always spoke as though he had authority. He not only interpreted but subsumed the law within his teaching of the wisdom that lay behind it and that lies in one way or another behind every good and profitable teaching that humanity has ever heard or ever could hear.

He spoke differently, too. He did not set himself up against the Bible; he revered it and upheld it as much as the most observant of rabbis. Nevertheless, he treated it as a precious *vade mecum*, a manual behind which lay a wisdom he was uniquely fitted to provide.

The Jews were and have often been called "the People of the Book." When they had first experienced deportation and exile after the fall of Jerusalem to the Babylonians in 586 B.C., they wondered at first how they could worship their God Yahweh at all "in a foreign land," for like primitive peoples everywhere they had thought of the land and its god as inseparable. They discovered, however, that there was one thing they could take with them that needed no temple: their Sacred Writings. They carried these in their hearts and memorized much in their heads, for as in all pre-literate societies their circumstances fostered great powers of memory. Far from the homeland they might never again see, they could still sing their songs, recount the deeds of their fathers, and above all remember the commandments given them by Moses. Many people today find psychological satisfaction in bringing a few familiar objects with them from their homeland to the land of their adoption, a few pictures, perhaps, or an old table or chair. But the Jews learned to cherish above all else the Word they could carry around inside them, strengthening them, sustaining them and preserving for them their identity as a community.

Jesus knew all this. It was deep in his heritage. Yet he knew and often hinted that what he had to offer was far more precious than anything that could possibly be reduced to writing, even the Word of God itself. He offered the divine Wisdom that lies behind the Word, that even the Word cannot fully contain. To have a packet of your mother's letters all tied up in blue ribbon is a joy to any filial heart; but it cannot be compared to having your mother in person. Jesus personified the divine Wisdom. That was what his diligent hearers sooner or later perceived.

One of the most striking features of Jesus as he comes to us in the Gospels is an uncanny ability to penetrate to the psychic core of every situation he encounters. Whatever methods he may have employed in teaching and in healing, he is clearly endowed with extraordinary powers of perception. He grasps total situations in a flash. He disarms people when he so chooses. Sometimes he heals; sometime he declines to do so. He frequently withdraws to pray in solitude as though recharging in himself the divine energy that he seems to store in such superabundance throughout his wanderings. Above all, he evokes from many their undying love and from some fear and relentless opposition.

Unlike some religious teachers, he does not try to live as though he were really not in the world. He is very much in the world; yet he is unmistakably bringing to it another dimension of being. More than anything else we see in Jesus is that ability to enrich life by adding another dimension rather than depriving it of the dimensions it already has. He uses astonishingly simple imagery: flowers, harvests, houses, parents, children, trees, pieces of money, lamps, and scores of other images close to the daily life of the people with whom he is involved. Yet everything he talks about becomes immediately invested with new significance. He does not merely expound the Wisdom of God; he exhibits it. He does not talk of the past except to bring into focus the nature of the reality of the present. Whatever he touches he irradiates with a mysterious light.

What, then, do the four Gospels really tell us about Jesus? It is not so much that an historical kernel remains after critical scholarship has torn off all else; it is rather that through a maze of history and theology the authoritative voice of the Eternal rings out and the persistent image of its lone spokesman passes before our eyes. Wherever he goes, he purifies and heals. What he does is what all good men wish to do; what he says is what all wise men have tried to say. Yet no one ever did things as he did them, and "Never man spake like this man." (John 7.46 KJV.)

The accounts we have do not give us a clear picture; nor can any amount of scholarly erudition and skill make them yield one; yet through them emerges a profoundly human figure who is at the same time uniquely superhuman. He transforms men and women, outcasts and sinners, even as he eats and drinks with them. He gathers disciples who accompany him on his travels; yet despite their presence, their conversation, and their questioning, he seems somehow to be always alone, beyond, above, and beneath whatever he did or said as he walked or sat, ate or drank, rejoiced or suffered, lived or died.

However he is depicted, something is always missing from even the most sensitive presentations of his life and work, making even the best of them seem caricatures. This is not merely because we want to idealize him, making him over to our own liking. To be sure, that has certainly been done over and over again. We all know the travesties that have been created: the gentle Jesus; the social revolutionary; the political agitator; the religious rebel; and many more. It is not only these foolish caricatures that he eludes and transcends, but even the most careful delineations of critical scholarship illumined by experience and prayer. Neither his words nor his deeds are unique; nor do the New Testament documents ever say they are. Far from it. He gives his disciples power to heal and "cast out devils" in his name and charges them to go out and teach what he taught. What he does is therefore reproducible and what he says is repeatable. In the Book of Acts the apostles of the Christian Way go on doing wonders such as he did and teaching the things he taught. Yet that is not the heart of their message. The heart of their message (the *kerygma*, the proclamation) is that Jesus, who has been crucified, "is risen" and lives. They speak not *about* what he preached or did; they are preaching *him*. Wherein, then, lies his uniqueness?

The uniqueness of Jesus lies not in what he says or in what he does but in what he is. If we discern anything at all in the records the four Evangelists provide, it is that Jesus is human like ourselves, wise like the wise among us and learned like the learned; yet he has the secret of all learning and wisdom and healing. All others, like John the Baptist, witness to the light; Jesus, by contrast, *is* the light. He is not merely in touch with the source of light and love; he *is* that source. So he can say in the language of his day and in terms of the religious tradition into which he was born, "I and my Father are one." (John 10.30.) That is the focus of orthodox Christian belief: the Eternal Logos was made flesh, encamped among us for a while, and lives and reigns forever in the hearts and minds of all who have been irradiated with his divine light.

APPENDIX 1

IS THE SHROUD OF TURIN AUTHENTIC?

We cannot overemphasize the fact, already noted, that the Christian Way was founded on the belief of the first apostles that Jesus "rose from the dead." "If Christ has not been raised," says Paul, "then our preaching is useless and your believing it is useless.... If our hope in Christ has been for this life only, we are the most unfortunate of all people." (I Corinthians 15.14, 19.) This was the essence of all the apostles had to say. Apart from the Resurrection, anything they might have said about Jesus would have been indeed worthless.

In view of the centrality of the resurrection to the whole history of the Christian Way, anything that might be at all connected with it acquires special relevance to our subject. That is why the legend of the Holy Shroud of Turin merits our attention. Everyone knows that false claims about religious relics abound. There are probably more alleged relics of the Cross than could ever have been hewn out of the amount of timber it contained. To many a saint has been ascribed more clothing than he or she could have worn. The legend of the Holy Shroud, however, is singular. Although its authenticity has been by no

201

means historically and scientifically established, a remarkable amount of scientific evidence has emerged in the last decade or two that either points to its authenticity or at least warrants our seriously entertaining it as a possibility. In the short bibliography at the end of this Appendix are a few of the studies that have been made by serious scholarly and scientific inquirers.

The relic, preserved at Turin since 1578, purports to be the winding-sheet in which the body of Jesus was wrapped for burial. It bears on front and back the positive imprint of the front and back of a human body, marked with the print of nails in the wrists and feet. Sophisticated modern cameras can discern and reproduce an image much clearer than the one on the cloth itself. This should not surprise us when we reflect that an ordinary X-Ray machine detects and puts on film certain vital information that is ordinarily invisible. The human eye can perceive wave-lengths only within an extremely limited range, as the human ear can hear only sounds within a similarly circumscribed range. I cannot hear sounds my dog can hear, for his range is different from mine; nor can I see what infra-red camera film can show me. Modern instruments can detect light that is invisible to the human eye. The face and body of Jesus on the cloth itself are not very lifelike; they *become* so through the aid of modern technology.

As already noted in Section 138, one hindrance to the full investigation has been the reluctance of the authorities at Turin to allow a Carbon 14 test, which would have damaged a substantial area of the material. Nevertheless, other tests have produced highly interesting results that make the notion of a medieval fraud much less credible than it might have been before modern investigations. Professor Max Frei, a Swiss criminologist, claims to have found pollen fossils from Turkey dating from the time of the Crusades. He has gone so far as to report, "I can state with certainty that the Turin Shroud dates from the time of Christ." Although not all scientific inquirers would concede this, testimony of this kind is certainly noteworthy. Dr. John H. Heller, however, a noted biophysicist, claims that pollen grains from plants unique to the south of Florida have been found as far north as Albany, New York.

The reference to Turkey is of special interest because of the possible identification of the Shroud with the legend of Abgar, King of Edessa. Edessa was an important site from very ancient times. The present city (now Urfa) was founded by Seleucus I in 304 B.C. From a very early date in the Christian era it became the center of the Syriac-speaking Christians. According to legend, a portrait of Christ miraculously imprinted on canvas was preserved there. The story was generally repudiated in the Christian West but accepted in the Christian East. The image of Edessa is believed to have been hidden and taken to Constantinople in the middle of the tenth century. It seems to have disappeared about the time the Crusaders sacked Constantinople in 1204. The connection is tenuous; nevertheless, any evidence suggesting that the Shroud of Turin has a Constantinopolitan ancestry does raise the question of a possible link. St. Catherine of Siena (14th century) mentions the Shroud in a letter, associating it with the East. Of course, not even a positive identification with the first century of the Christian era would prove its authenticity as the winding-sheet of Jesus. A first-century dating would, however, virtually demolish all forgery theories.

How could the Shroud have received the imprint of the face and body of Jesus, if indeed the relic is authentic? Is not the Gospel testimony itself incompatible with the legend? By no means. The practice was (and it has persisted down to modern times) to bind the face with a cloth tied round the chin and head to prevent an unsightly sagging jaw, which happens when a corpse is left untended. Bandages might also be used to keep other parts of the body in place.

We recall that the rich friend of Jesus, Joseph of Arimathaea, brought seventy pounds of myrrh and aloes for the anointing of Jesus's body. Linen by itself is a comparatively stiff, unyielding material; but if the grave were plastered with these spices and the body saturated with them, the linen would presumably cling to the body and the myrrh and aloes together might very well release a dye that would produce an imprint such as is found on the Shroud. The notion that ammonia vapors had combined with the myrrh and aloes to create a negative image on the cloth is, however, widely discredited today. The team of experts who examined the Shroud in Turin in 1978 found no trace of myrrh or aloes. Dr. Walter McCrone, a Chicago microanalyst, who takes the Shroud to be a fake, claims to have found red oxide on the cloth. On the other hand, Robert Bucklin, deputy medical examiner for Los Angeles County, is favorably disposed to the view that the Shroud might be authentic.

Another theory, not incompatible with this "contact" one, is the "scorch" or "burn" theory that release of an extraordinary energy, a flash of light at the moment of resurrection occurring with nuclear force, might result in what we have in the Shroud of Turin.

Much more striking is the positive evidence that a Jesuit professor at Loyola University of Chicago has recently brought to bear upon the Shroud. This Jesuit scholar, Father Francis L. Filas, had for some time claimed to identify a coin mark on the eyes, which he took to be a Roman one of about the period in question. (Coins have been used in early times along with the head bandage, and for similar cosmetic reasons. The weight of the coins over the closed eyes prevents them from remaining fixed in a fearsome stare. Down to the present century, indeed, the British used the old large pennies for this purpose.) Then in October 1979 Bill Yarborough of East Point, Georgia, a numismatist, gave Father Filas a coin. In August 1981, when a 22-time englargement of the coin was made for television, Father Filas noticed that a misspelling occurred in letters only 1.3 millimeters high. The coin, issued in the reign of Tiberius, showed the first letters of the Greek word *Kaisaros* (Emperor) erroneously spelt *Caisaros*. Numismatists know that Pontius Pilate issued coins of this type no earlier than A.D. 29 and for only two or three years thereafter. Then came a startling discovery: Father Filas, who by digital analysis had found the pattern of a coin over the eyes on the Shroud markings, made a photographic enlargement of the imprint on the Shroud, which revealed a coin pattern so exactly corresponding to that of the coin he had acquired that he was able to superimpose the one over the other on a projection screen so that they coincided, including the misspelling — an extremely rare minting error. Father Filas's report certainly seems to make any suggestion of medieval forgery exceedingly difficult to maintain. Indeed to say this must surely be accounted by many an overcautious understatement.

Suggested Reading

The literature of the Holy Shroud of Turin is growing rapidly. One of the best accounts of the history and scientific investigation of the Shroud, although now becoming in some respects outdated because of the extensive work done since its publication, is:

Werner Bulst, S.J., *The Shroud of Turin* (trans. S. McKenna and J. J. Galvin). Milwaukee: Bruce Publishing Company, 1957.

It has an excellent bibliography classified both according to date and according to viewpoint (for or against authenticity), and there is an interesting discussion of the manner in which the body of Jesus may have been laid out (pp. 77-101). The text is copiously illustrated.

Also useful are the following:

Rodney Hoare, *The Testimony of the Shroud*. London Quartet Books, 1978.

J. Walsh, *The Shroud*. London: W. H. Allen, 1964.

An especially useful recent work is:

Ian Wilson, *The Shroud of Turin*. New York:Doubleday and Company, Inc., 1978.

Wilson discusses in detail the connection between the Shroud and the Mandylion that disappeared during the Crusaders' sack of Constantinople in 1204, with persuasive arguments for identifying them.

Another recent work, which contains an account of the author's extensive travels and interviews with sindonologists and others, and written in a somewhat racy style is:

Robert K. Wilcox, *Shroud*. New York: The Macmillan Company, 1977.

Wilcox, who provides a bibliography, has sections on the "contact stain" theory (pp. 63ff.) and the "scorch" theory (pp. 125ff.).

A pioneer modern work by Paul Vignon has been handsomely produced in a new form in English translation:

Paul Vignon, *The Shroud of Christ*. New Hyde Park, New York: University Books, 1970.

The results of the investigation by this author, a *docteur-ès-sciences* and a believer, were presented to the French Academy of Sciences by his agnostic friend Dr. Yves Delage. The *Académie* declined to print Vignon's paper. *The Lancet*, however, favorably reviewed it.

For a semi-popular account of current medical disagreement on the Shroud, see:

R. W. Rhein, Jr., "The Shroud of Turin," in *Medical World News* (McGraw Hill), December 22, 1980, pp. 40-50.

The Holy Shroud Information Centre, 58 Harrow Road, West Bridgford, Nottingham, England, publishes a booklet by D. Allen-Griffiths, *Whose Image and Likeness?* The author is a perfervid believer in the Shroud's authenticity.

The literature is growing so rapidly, however, that any bibliography is quickly outdated.

APPENDIX II

THE TEXT OF THE BIBLE
AND ITS INTERPRETATION

The English Bible as we know it today comes in many versions and translations. The history of the making of the English Bible and of the original documents that lie behind it has been treated in numerous books, including two of my own.[1] We need note here only some basic facts. There were already several versions of the English Bible even before the publication in 1611 of what is now probably the best known, the King James Version. One of these, William Tyndale's revision of his translation of the New Testament, published in 1534, was the first printed New Testament in English. It improved considerably upon Wyclif's, which had circulated in manuscript in the fourteenth century before the invention in Europe of printing by movable type. Since then an enormous number of English versions and translations have been printed, some good, some bad, some indifferent, right down to the present day.

[1]E.g., *The Bible In the Making* (Philadelphia: J. B. Lippincott Company, 1959 and London: John Murray, 1961), which contains an account for general readers.

The King James Version was in its day a magnificent work in which forty-seven of the best biblical scholars in England were engaged. Its style was superb, intentionally just a little old-fashioned even when that version appeared. It soon acquired repute over all its competitors. It remained supreme for two hundred and fifty years and has remained very influential down to our own time. Unfortunately, however, various scholarly finds occurring just after its appearance (including the arrival in England of one of the earliest manuscripts of the Greek text, the Codex Alexandrinus), rendered it soon outdated from a scholarly standpoint. Today there are several excellent versions and translations, including the Jerusalem Bible, from which I have generally quoted in the present book.

Behind the English Bible lies a long ancestry going back to the Hebrew of the Old Testament and the Greek of the New Testament. Several versions of the Greek text are in existence. The oldest, fairly complete manuscripts of the Greek New Testament are the Codex Vaticanus, in the Vatican Library, and the Codex Sinaiticus, in the British Museum. The latter, discovered by a German scholar, Constantin Tischendorf, who visited the monastery of St. Catherine on Mount Sinai in May, 1844, was acquired by the Tsar of Russia and placed in the Imperial Library. After the Bolshevik Revolution in 1917, it passed into the hands of the Soviet Government, from which it was purchased in 1933 for the British Museum at the price of £100,000, at that time about half a million dollars: even then an excellent bargain. Both these manuscripts date from the fourth century. Other ancient manuscripts include the Codex Alexandrinus, also in the British Museum and dating from the early fifth century, and the Codex Ephraemi, a fifth-century manuscript now in the Bibliothèque Nationale, Paris. Thousands of earlier fragments, however, and much other relevant material have been discovered, including the great finds at Qumran and also the Nag Hammadi Library, both about the middle of the present century.

No such ancient manuscripts of the Hebrew Bible survive. Several reasons account for this fact. One is the comparative dampness of the Palestinian soil, less conducive to the preservation of papyrus than the dry soil of Egypt. More significant is the fact that when, after the fall of the Temple in Jerusalem in the year A.D. 70, the dispersed Jews carried their Bibles with them, they developed such exacting standards for copying that copies meeting these standards were comparatively rare. Probably the most important reason of all is that as soon as any scroll became worn out it had to be discarded and eventually burned. The Jews had no interest in preserving old tattered copies of the Hebrew Bible when they could make new ones with a text whose accuracy was assured by the rigid standards in force. So except for partial manuscripts, notably the Qumran scroll of the Book of Isaiah, which dates from about the time of Jesus (perhaps even earlier), the oldest manuscripts of then Hebrew Bible known to exist cannot be dated earlier than about A.D. 900. Because of the extreme care in copying, however, we can be assured of remarkable accuracy in the text that has come down to us. Evidence of this is provided by the fact that when, for example, that very ancient scroll of Isaiah was made accessible to scholars, they could find no significant deviations from the text previously available to them.

By contrast, New Testament scribes were often notably careless, so that textual scholars have to examine every available manuscript to determine, as far as possible, the text we are to accept as "most correct." Through such diligence, however, we may be reasonably certain that the text as now accepted in scholarly circles is very close indeed to what the New Testament writers wrote. Accuracy is not determined only through examination of manuscripts of the Greek text. Some of the Old Latin texts, for instance, are very ancient indeed and can provide corroborative evidence.

The text of the Hebrew Bible had already been subjected to editorial processes before the time of Jesus and indeed the "canon" or approved list of the books it was to contain was not finally fixed until A.D. 70. The Jews venerated above all the Torah or Law (the first five books of the Bible), then the Prophets, which came second in esteem, and finally the rest, which are called the Writings and include books such as the Psalms and Job. Orthodox Jews to this day will take care not only that nothing is placed on top of a copy of the Bible but that the Bible itself is so laid down that the lesser books are not sitting on the top of the Torah.

The importance of the Bible for the Jews was enormously enhanced by the fact that when Jerusalem fell in 586 B.C., sending thousands into exile in Babylon, the Jews found themselves with nothing of their religion save their Scriptures. You cannot carry a temple with you, but you can carry the Word and keep it even in your head. Then when Alexander the Great expelled the Persian armies from Asia Minor and Syria, he took Palestine on his way to Egypt where he founded the city of Alexandria. That great city, as he had hoped, became a world center for the spread of hellenistic culture and the Greek way of life. Within a few generations upper class Jews from Palestine, including priests, were much influenced by Greek thought. Thousands migrated to Alexandria and were further affected by hellenic ways. Many forgot their Hebrew. The need for a translation of the Bible into Greek was met by a version begun in the third century B.C. in Alexandria, known to scholars as the Septuagint, from a legend that seventy translators were engaged upon it.

The Septuagint is extremely important for a scholarly understanding of the Bible. It is the version that the New Testament writers used when they quoted passages from the ancient Scriptures. It also contains a number of books not found in the Hebrew canon. These books include much of the Wisdom literature, which has great theosophical significance, for instance, the Wisdom of Solomon and the Wisdom of Sirach (sometimes called Ecclesiasticus, contradistinguished from Ecclesiastes, which is in the Hebrew canon). These books are also found in the Vulgate, the Latin version used by the Roman Catholic Church, and are also venerated by Anglicans. For historical reasons, however, they have been omitted from versions and translations of the Bible done under Protestant auspices. They are naturally an important part of the biblical heritage of Eastern Orthodox Christians.

It is very important for us to appreciate the enormous influence of Hellenistic thought on Judaism in the centuries immediately preceding the birth of Jesus. Books such as Job and the Wisdom literature reflect this cosmopolitan outlook that would have been inconceivable in pre-exilic Hebrew society. The Jews of the Diaspora, dispersed throughout the Mediterranean world and elsewhere, had been exposed, by the time of Jesus, to these cosmopolitan influences. They would be in many cases almost as different from their Palestinian counterparts as would a modern inhabitant of New York of English ancestry be from his or her counterpart in a ninteenth-century English village. The Greek language, which in its *koinē* form served as an international medium somewhat as does English today, immensely helped in hellenizing these Diaspora Jews. Even to the extremely conservative, not to say narrow and clannish, society of Jews in Palestine, Greek influences penetrated. A people under an army of occupation cannot but learn some of the language of their conquerors, and with the language are learned some of the ideas. Moreover, it seems to have been the practice for foreign armies of occupation in Palestine to be billeted in private homes rather than in barracks, which would inevitably engender interchange. Religions as well as other ideas would travel, even in such a walled-off society as that of Palestinian Jewry.

When all these circumstances are taken into account we can more easily appreciate that, contrary to a belief once widely held in certain circles, the Judaism into which Jesus was born already had been long exposed to cosmopolitan influences. It is even likely that Jesus would know some Greek, although his ordinary tongue was Aramaic (an outgrowth of classical Hebrew). The Greek-speaking audiences Paul met on his missionary travels throughout the Mediterranean, Jewish as well as Gentile, would of course be very much exposed to such cosmopolitan religious ideas.

The interpretation of the Bible is nowadays an extremely complex and learned enterprise whose intricacies are recognized by the best scholars in all traditions—Christian and Jewish, Catholic and Protestant, Eastern Orthodox and Anglican. Scholars apply to the Bible the same basic principles of literary criticism that are brought to Shakespeare and other literature. Any useful attempt to interpret the Bible requires and ought to presuppose a basic training in the professional skills and the methodology of literary, including biblical, exegesis. Yet in addition to the use of these general principles (a very technical business), scholars are also very much aware of the special character and complexity of the literature we call the Bible. This literature, like the Hindu and Buddhist Scriptures, was written over a long period of time (about a thousand years in the case of the Bible), and much edited before reaching anything like the form in which we now know it. To say this is by no means necessarily to deny that the Bible is "divinely inspired," although what precisely such a phrase means is an obvious question. Certainly the Bible is not a book to be read through as having the logical sequence of a well-written history, biography, epic, or play. It is, rather, a miscellany of literature bearing upon the traffic between God and man.

Yet when all that is said, we must also recognize another consideration. Even the most learned and competent biblical scholars bring to their work their own personal experience and their own special viewpoints. In this they are not different from other literary critics. Shakespearian scholars also inevitably bring to their task their own special conditions and attitudes of mind. Not all, for instance, would see in *Hamlet* the parapsychological elements that some would account both so obvious and so illuminating. Technical training is essential,

214

if only to save us from forming foolish opinions that are demonstrably incapable of being proven and further of wasting time on enterprises that cannot possibly be fruitful. Nevertheless, more is needed than technical expertise, vital as that is. We must *also* bring to the task our own personal experience, our own wisdom. The classic Protestant theologians recognized this in their own way when they insisted on bringing to the reading of the Bible the "testimony of the Holy Spirit," while Catholic theologians have also recognized it in their emphasis on exhibiting the Bible always in the light of the Church's life. Spiritually sensitive people will bring to the Bible the insights they have always brought to it.

We should bear in mind that the Bible is as basic to all forms of Christian thought and all styles of Christian life as is the United States Constitution to all aspects of American society. Apart from the Bible, every Christian tradition would collapse. It is the ground on which all Christian teaching stands, whether orthodox or heterodox, Protestant or Catholic. But what precisely is the Bible? Textually, what Christians acknowledge and revere is the Bible that is recognized by Jews, with the addition of twenty-seven other books that Christians traditionally call the New Testament. These additional books consist mainly of a number of letters written by Paul and others to communities and individuals following the Christian Way and scattered throughout the Mediterranean lands, along with the Apocalypse or Revelation and four presentations of the Gospel. One of these, attributed to John, stands very much by itself; the other three (Matthew, Mark, Luke), are called "the Synoptic Gospels." The Gospels, despite the special importance Christians attach to them, are by no means the earliest literature in the New Testament. Much earlier are Paul's letters, some of which were written possibly within twenty years of the Crucifixion of Jesus.

The Gospels, like the rest of the Bible, must be interpreted in one way or another, although always with the scholarly tools that are indispensable to any biblical scholar. Christians interpret the whole Bible, Old Testament and New, with Jesus Christ as its focus, so the Gospels are of special importance to them. No Jew or Muslim, however great his respect for Jesus, could so interpret the Bible, nor could anyone who did not first take a specifically Christian perspective. We must see, however, precisely what a Christian perspective entails. To do this we must have some understanding of the climate of thought and the circumstances of life prevailing when the Christian Way first became a viable option for both Jews and Gentiles in the Mediterranean world.

Of one thing we may be certain. The text by itself is lifeless. It is "the spirit" that gives life (John 6.63). We are entitled to take a stance, so long as such a stance is grounded in cogent and informed exegesis. Christian scholars deem a Christian stance not only academically respectable but peculiarly fruitful. We must respect the claim that such a perspective yields an especially rich understanding of the divine wisdom ("the Word of God") contained in the Bible and revealed or unfolded to those who have "ears to hear." (Matthew 11.15.) Christianity, for all the evils done in its name, has wielded an extraordinary influence on human society in the course of two thousand years, not only in the West but to some extent elsewhere. It may be said to have cradled a unique kind of civilization and culture. Some would even contend that it was the catalyst that set in motion the seventeenth-century developments leading to modern scientific methods and procedures and issuing in the technological discoveries that have revolutionized life in the West. Be that as it may, it is certainly by any reckoning a tremendous clearing house for religious ideas, functioning therefore in the West somewhat as does Hinduism in the East.

The most learned modern biblical scholars, when they approach the Gospels, are by no means insensitive to hidden motifs, especially in their understanding of the parables and other such features of the Gospels as we know them. No one who knows anything about the nature of the New Testament literature can suppose that the Gospels provide a ''life of Jesus'' in the sense of a modern biography. For nobody in those days wrote the sort of work that is expected of a modern biographer. Such a literary *genre* simply did not exist. What scholars do argue about is the extent to which anything like a realistic life of Jesus can be reconstructed from the biblical materials. In the ''quest for the historical Jesus'' made repeatedly during this century, some scholars have felt able to extract a good deal of solid information about Jesus, while others have felt that we can see at best mere glimpses of him through a very heavy veil. All have recognized, however, that old-fashioned ways of reading the Gospels as though they were straightforward accounts of the life and teachings of Jesus were, although well-intentioned in their day, extremely misguided, misleading, and unprofitable. They have seen the need for digging for hidden wisdom and for the unravelling of many mysteries within the sacred page.

We may well ask, however, whether even such modern exegesis has gone far enough in unearthing the living wisdom within the dead page. Those who acknowledge that such methods are on the right lines would be the first to deny that there is no room for deeper discernment. On the contrary, what is revealed discloses that much is concealed. I cannot tell you half a secret without your becoming more than ever aware, if you have any imagination at all, that something has been hidden from you.

Christians claim that Jesus Christ is ''the full and final revelation'' of God to man. But what precisely does this mean? Have Christians always appropriated that revelation in its fullness? Might it even be that Christians have hardly ever so appropriated it? Christians also recognize that what is revealed of the nature of God in the Person of Jesus the Christ was only partially hidden before it was revealed; otherwise it would make no sense to talk of his being ''the full revelation'' of God. Moreover, the claim that Jesus Christ is ''the full and final revelation" of God to man does not assert anything about his being "the full and final revelation" of God to the inhabitants of other planets.

That the writers of the New Testament, not least Paul and John, were deeply influenced by the Gnostic, theosophical ideas of their age has become increasingly clear in recent decades by biblical scholarship. That is not to say by any means that they swallowed and expounded all theosophical ideas that happened to come their way. On the contrary, they patently rejected some and selected others, transmogrifying many of the ideas with which they, along with the rest of the Mediterranean world, were familiar. They lived and thought, however, in an atmosphere saturated with such ideas. To try to understand the Gospels apart from such a climate of thought is like trying to understand medieval European art without knowing anything about Catholicism.

Perhaps a word should be said here about the concept of "reading the Bible literally." The notion that people in the past habitually did so and have only recently read it otherwise is a crassly ignorant one. Not only did the early Christian Fathers, notably the Alexandrians, read the Bible allegorically; the men of the Middle Ages were so inclined to allegorize in reading the biblical books that from time to time they were recalled (by the Victorine school, for instance) to pay attention to what the text actually says. No literature with any literary content in it richer than that of the telephone directory can be adequately read without some allegorization. This is much more conspicuously the case with religious literature. Only a singularly irreligious person could try to read the Bible or any other religious literature literally.

In this book we have examined the life and work of Jesus as presented in the four Gospels, harmonizing the parallels in such a way as to try to get a perspective of the life and teaching of Jesus. As has been emphasized from the outset, we are not to suppose, for instance, that the "Sermon on the Mount" was ever delivered as a single oration to a specific assembly of hearers, for that,

to say the least, is very unlikely. It was much more probably composed as a compilation of his typical sayings,
many of which he may possibly have uttered in the
course of this or that discourse. Nor need we be particularly concerned in all cases with the sequence of events,
if only because trying to establish any such sequence is
often at best a highly precarious enterprise and probably
a futile one. Nor again are we to worry whether or not a
particular incident, such as the encounter with the
Samaritan woman at the well, occurred exactly as reported, or even that it occurred at all. Yet that is not to
say that we are to be free to disregard the historicity of the
Gospels altogether, as though it did not matter whether
Jesus ever existed. We know almost nothing about the life
of Socrates except what has come down to us through
Plato, for like Jesus he wrote nothing for posterity to read.
From the Gospels we can form a general picture of the
kind of person Jesus was, of the nature of his life, and of
the basic points of his teaching.

To read the Gospels, however, as if the setting were
a contemporary one in which the characters were thinking and talking in typical twentieth-century terms is a
notoriously foolish error. When, for example, Jesus is
reported as talking of "the world" (*ho kosmos*), the term
is not a morally neutral one as it would be in ordinary
conversation today; it means a realm of spiritual slavery,
the realm in which, for one reason or another, we are
currently immersed. It is a familiar Gnostic notion that
the world as we know it is evil. When Jesus speaks of
"the prince of this world" (*ho tou kosmou arxōn*) who
"is on his way" (e.g., John 14.30), he means Satan, the
chief of the evil spirits or demonic forces who, impeding
the divine light, keep the world in darkness, thereby
subjecting men and women to bondage and spiritual
death. In such a condition men and women are blind. Not
only are they watching shadow-play like the men in
Plato's allegory of the Cave; their blindness corrupts
all their thoughts, their words, and their acts. They belong to the realm of darkness. In some Gnostic teaching

the original state of the world is depicted like this. According to John, the world is not so created; it is the creation of the one true God, Him who is the source of all light and life. Nevertheless, the contrast between this Source of all good and the "prince of this world" remains. Light and darkness, life and death: these are the categories in which John deals over and over, reflecting both the customary ways of thinking, which derived from the Ancient Wisdom, and his own originality in interpreting the situation.

As we have studied each story, parable, and saying, we have seen hidden meanings in the life and work of Jesus. While these are often easy for any spiritually minded person to perceive, they often go deeper than might be expected even by such an enlightened reader. Of course exegetes have always known that a search for hidden meanings such as we are proposing is fraught with many kinds of danger. To neglect to attempt it at all, however, would be to guarantee the stunting of our inner growth.

Suggested Reading

For a study of the history of attempts to provide the story of Jesus's life, the classic work is:

Albert Schweitzer, *The Quest of the Historical Jesus.* New York: The Macmillan Company, 1961. Translated by W. Montgomery from the first German edition, *Von Reimarus zu Wrede*, 1906. New introduction by J. M. Robinson.

The bibliography is enormous and new forms of the old quest continue to be made with the scholarly tools of today. A convenient and useful anthology of important scholarly writings on the subject (including representative passages from T. W. Manson, G. Bornkamm, V. Taylor, C. H. Dodd, C. K. Barrett, R. G. Fuller, E. Stauffer, J. Jeremias, R. Bultmann, S. Sandmel, P. Tillich, Van A. Harvey, J. Knox, J. S. Stewart, O. Cullmann, B. Gerhardsson, X. Leon-Dufour, R. E. Brown, and Wikenhauser) is:

H. K. McArthur (ed.), *In Search of the Historical Jesus.* New York: Charles Scribner's Sons, 1969.

For the geography and archeology of physical sites relating to the life of Jesus, an excellent book, copiously illustrated, is:

Jack Finegan, *The Archeology of the New Testament.* Princeton: Princeton University Press, 1969.

The discovery of manuscripts and fragments in Egypt and elsewhere, which has been progressing from the beginning of the present century—and especially the great finds at Qumran and Nag Hammadi—has inevitably stimulated a lively interest in Gnosticism. Even the most conservative scholars have been forced to revise traditional views of the role of Gnostic ideas in primitive Christianity. Not only were Gnostic ideas far more influential in early Christian thought than had been traditionally supposed; scholars are increasingly appreciating that Christianity was deeply rooted in a Gnostic background. That is not to say, of course, that all Gnostic ideas were consonant with Christian thought. That would be almost like saying, a thousand years from now, that all twentieth-century philosophy was compatible with twentieth-century religious belief. Gnosticism took many forms. What is becoming clear is that Christianity was cradled in Gnosticism and what both Jesus and Paul taught was a special form of that Ancient Wisdom. The student interested in pursuing the consequences of this development in the study of Christian origins and of the life and work of Jesus should consult a work of my own, which contains a considerable bibliography of books and articles on Gnosticism:

Geddes MacGregor, *Gnosis: A Renaissance in Christian Thought.* Wheaton, Illinois: The Theosophical Publishing House (Quest Books), 1979.

There are many admirable books on the text of the Bible and its interpretation, some of which deal also with the history of the English Bible. Another work of mine is helpful for the general reader:

Geddes MacGregor: *The Bible in the Making.* Philadelphia and New York: J. B. Lippincott Company, 1959.

Among modern classics on the Bible for more advanced and technically trained students may be mentioned:

Rudolf Bultmann, *Theology of the New Testament* (trans. K. Grobel; 2 volumes). New York: Charles Scribner's Sons, 1951 and 1955.

Joachim Jeremias, *The Parables of Jesus* (trans. S. H. Hooke). New York: Charles Scribner's Sons, 1963.

Joachim Jeremias, *New Testament Theology* (trans. J. Bowden). New York: Charles Scribner's Sons, 1971.

F. F. Bruce, *New Testament History*. New York: Doubleday and Company, Inc., 1971.

W. D. Davies, *Invitation to the New Testament*. New York: Doubleday and Company, Inc., Anchor Books edition, 1969.

Klaus Koch, *The Growth of the Biblical Tradition* (trans. S. M. Cupitt). New York: Charles Scribner's Sons, 1969.

Reginald H. Fuller, *The New Testament in Current Study*. New York: Charles Scribner's Sons, 1962.

Reincarnation in Christianity

Geddes MacGregor is the author of the much acclaimed Quest book *Reincarnation in Christianity* in which he questions whether or not there is room for the doctrine of reincarnation in Christian dogma. He asks, "Can Christians possibly accept the rebirth concept while remaining loyal to Bible and church?"

Students of religion, scholars, and laymen alike, will welcome this exhaustive inquiry. It provides a long needed, long awaited critical examination of the pros and cons of this question. Dr. MacGregor cuts through centuries of emotional hyperbole and narrow dogma and analytically reports important comments by some of the world's greatest Christian figures. He offers philosophical, scientific, and Biblical "for and against" evidence for support of his appraisal.

"Professor MacGregor's exciting thesis challenges our traditional orthodoxy."—*Cardinal Manning, Archbishop of Los Angeles.*

Another book by Dr. MacGregor is called
Gnosis

". . . a mood is widespread," writes Dr. MacGregor, "that is unfavorable to religious dogmatism but favorable to the exploration of what lies behind the dogmas." With this in mind, the author provides us with a contemporary look at the controversial system of thought known as *gnosticism*, a way of understanding Christianity that was integral to this religion early in its history.

Available from QUEST BOOKS
306 W. Geneva Road   Wheaton, Illinois 60187